Handbook of
English Mediaeval Costume

also by C. Willett Cunnington

★

ENGLISH WOMEN'S CLOTHING IN THE
NINETEENTH CENTURY
ENGLISH WOMEN'S CLOTHING IN THE
PRESENT CENTURY
WHY WOMEN WEAR CLOTHES
FEMININE FIGLEAVES

★

by C. W. and Phillis Cunnington
THE HISTORY OF UNDERCLOTHES
(Michael Joseph)

FRONTISPIECE (13th Century)
Embroidered tunic with typical 13th century
'magyar' sleeves. Fur-lined mantle. Decorative soled hose.

HANDBOOK OF
ENGLISH MEDIAEVAL
COSTUME

by

C. Willett & Phillis
CUNNINGTON

with illustrations by
BARBARA PHILLIPSON

FABER AND FABER LIMITED
24 Russell Square
London

First published in mcmlii
by Faber and Faber Limited
24 Russell Square London W.C.1
Printed in Great Britain by
R. MacLehose and Company Limited
The University Press Glasgow

Contents

Preface

The aim of this Handbook is to present in a concise form a systematic account of English Mediaeval Costume, from A.D. 800 to A.D. 1500.

The material has been obtained from illustrations in illuminated MSS., church effigies, brasses, and from contemporary literature. We have availed ourselves of the extensive researches by those authors mentioned in the bibliography, and to whom we are much indebted. We also wish to thank the Essex Archaeological Society, whose invaluable library at Colchester has been of very great help, the Essex Record Office, Chelmsford, and the authorities in charge of the British Museum Library, the Victoria and Albert Museum Library, The John Rylands Library, Manchester, the Fitzwilliam Museum, Cambridge, the Trinity College Library, Cambridge, Colchester Castle Museum, Peterborough Museum, Durham Cathedral Library, Exeter Cathedral Library, Hereford Cathedral Library, and Ripon Cathedral Library.

Care has been taken to check all dates from contemporary sources; and those given indicate the limits of a 'fashion', though doubtless exceptions occur outside these limits. The line drawings, made under our supervision, serve to clarify verbal descriptions. Some foreign sources have been preferred to English ones where they provided clearer illustrations of identical fashions. Thus a 'butterfly headdress' is better understood in a foreign picture than in an English brass. The coloured illustrations are intended to represent the types of colour schemes employed, and do not profess to be replicas of originals.

The nomenclature used by mediaeval writers was confusing, often with names applied to more than one garment, or with several names for one and the same thing. We have simplified this, and relegated to a glossary terms of uncertain or irregular use. In the description of the various garments we have included only those forms for which there is reliable evidence that they were in use in this country, and no positive fact has been stated which has not been confirmed from authentic sources.

As a reference book the arrangement of the material has been designed to facilitate accurate and ready dating of mediaeval illustrations, effigies, brasses, etc. It may also serve as a companion to the larger works on the subject and as a convenient guide to the stage costumier. For Underclothes see our 'History of Underclothes', 1951.

Foreign evidence is valuable provided that we allow for the 'time-lag' which elapsed, especially from the fourteenth century onwards, before such fashions were adopted here; and that we eliminate those which seem never to have crossed the Channel.

A single fragment of evidence must be accepted with caution. Thus in *Eulogium Historiarum* [c. 1420] is the statement so much copied by later writers, that the long toes of piked shoes (tempus Richard II) were even supported by chains to the knee. Fairholt, in his *Costume in England*, 1860, specifically stated that this fashion 'is well authenticated by contemporary narrators', but gave no references; and subsequent writers have entirely failed to discover any. It has been suggested that perhaps it was a mode displayed by the courtiers coming here with Anne of Bohemia. There seems no evidence that it became an *English* fashion, and we follow Mr Kelly in ignoring it.

Knitting was in use in the reign of Queen Mary.[1] Yet we find in the Household Accounts of Sir John Fastolf [c. 1450] mention of a 'knitted cap', and M. Harmand says he has found similar references in the fifteenth century. We do not know whether such isolated examples were 'foreign imports', but they cannot justifiably be described as a 'fashion'. We reserve that term for styles proved by contemporary evidence to have been in general use; while those which were less common—though not unique— we call 'rare'.

[1] (1557). 'Item pd for the knytting of ii paire of hosen for Mr. George Farmer 14d.' Essex Record Office (D.DP. A9c.)

Ninth and Tenth Centuries

MEN

1. THE TUNIC

A loose garment worn next to the shirt and put on over the head.

Length

(*a*) Short, about knee-length, and sometimes slit up at the sides.

(*b*) Long, ankle length, usually worn by nobility on ceremonial occasions.

Neck

(*a*) Round, with enough room for the head to pass.

(*b*) Round, with a short vertical slit in front.

(*c*) Square.

Sleeves

(*a*) Close fitting to wrist, usually with many circular puckers round forearm giving plenty of play. The sleeves were probably made to reach beyond the hand.

(*b*) Sometimes loose and open (with long tunics).

Girdles. Narrow sashes, almost invariably worn.

Embroidery. At neck, wrists, hem and girdle, in coloured silks, was common. Precious stones added for ceremonial garments.

Materials. Linen for the wealthy, wool for the poorer.

2. THE SUPER-TUNIC

'ROC' was the Saxon name (hence the word 'frock'). Worn over the tunic, was loose fitting and put on over the head through a wide neck opening.

1. 10TH CENTURY

(a) Long, square-necked tunic, over which is worn a draped mantle.
'Phrygian bonnet'. (b) Short tunic with close puckered sleeves.
Cloak clasped on right shoulder. Loose stockings. Shoes. (c) Metal
fillet. Embroidered neck of tunic. (d) Short tunic with girdle.
Alternate neck line.

Length

(*a*) Long, but revealing the bottom of the tunic. The long super-tunic was worn over the long ceremonial tunic by persons of rank, and was usually embroidered round the neck, sleeves and hem. Sometimes made of silk. Its sleeves were full and open to elbow or wrist; or, rarely, tight-fitting.

(*b*) Short. Sleeves tight-fitting to wrist, or, very rarely, loose.

Girdles. Optional with both forms.

3. THE CLOAK OR MANTLE

Cut on the square and not on a circle. Varied from a short cape to a long flowing mantle, the latter chiefly reserved for the nobility.

Worn over tunic or super-tunic.

Fastenings

(*a*) By brooch or clasp on right shoulder, leaving right arm free. Vice versa for left-handed men.

(*b*) By ties, brooch or clasp in front.

No Hoods (as in the twelfth century)

In the tenth century, the mantle in the shape of a large oblong shawl was sometimes worn wrapped round the body from the waist, forming a loose shapeless skirt, the free end being draped over the left or right shoulder.

4. THE DOUBLE MANTLE

Large and square, with a hole in the centre for slipping over the head. Worn without brooch or buckle. For men and women of the highest rank only. All mantles (particularly those worn by women) were often lined with material of a different colour, e.g. red lined with blue.

5. THE BRATT

A short coarse mantle worn by peasants, possibly a humble imitation of the 'Saga Tresonica' (a short French Cloak).

a

b

c

2. 9TH AND 10TH CENTURIES

(a) Long boots. (b) Short boots, decorated. (c) Leg bandages and shoes.

6. LEGWEAR

(1) BRAIES OR DRAWERS were moderately loose-fitting breeches, tied on just below the waist by a running string, and ending above or below the knee. If below they were somewhat close-fitting and secured by ties. Worn by all classes.

(2) TROUSERS were long drawers reaching to the ankles and sometimes slit up behind the calf. Often bound from knee to ankle with bandages. Worn by all classes.

(3) HOSE, corresponding to stockings, a word not used in this limited sense until the seventeenth century. To avoid confusion, however, the term will be used to indicate stockings as we know them.

Either long to thighs, usually worn by the rich, often made of linen. Or short, barely reaching the knees, and when of wool worn by the rustics and poorer classes.

Both kinds were often brightly coloured.

(4) SOCKS. Worn with trousers or sometimes over stockings; also often brightly coloured and having decorative borders.

(5) LEG BANDAGES were strips of linen or wool bound spirally over stockings or trousers from foot or ankle to just below the knee. The criss-cross arrangement was confined to royalty and high ecclesiastics. Their bandages were often embroidered.

Leg bandages might replace stockings, being worn like puttees with the ends tucked in at the top, or tied and left dangling if tasselled.

7. FOOTWEAR

(1) SHOES shaped to the foot, distinguishing right from left, and slightly pointed opposite the big toe. The raised heel was unknown throughout the Middle Ages.

Styles

(a) Fairly wide opening round ankle.

(b) Close round ankle, with central slit down the top of the foot.

(c) Close round ankle with side slits leaving a centre flap.

Fastenings

(a) By thongs attached behind, passed round the ankle and tied over instep in front.

(*b*) No fastenings.

Materials. Chiefly leather. Soles of leather or wood, and sometimes reinforced by studding with nails.

(2) BOOTS, reaching to mid-calf, or shorter. Loose or tied with thongs. Often decorated.

(3) WOODEN CLOGS sometimes worn.

(4) SLIPPERS, with open tops and low vamps, worn by the clergy and women.

8. HEADWEAR

(1) NONE. It was the fashion to go bareheaded.

(2) PLAIN METAL FILLETS.

(3) THE 'PHRYGIAN BONNET'. A small cap with a pointed crown curved forwards. A number of slight variations in shape and decoration occurred.

Worn until the beginning of the thirteenth century. *Materials.* Skins of animals, wool and felt.

9. HAIR

Young men wore thick hair waving back from the forehead and temples, sometimes with a short centre parting, to nape of neck or lower. Clean shaven face. Older men wore their hair waving down from a centre parting or a fringe, to neck or shoulders. Whiskers, moustaches, and long beards often forked and pointed, were usual.

10. ACCESSORIES

Wallets, slung from the shoulders or girdle.

Bracelets, generally of gold, and rings of gold or metal.

Shoulder Belts, passing over the right shoulder to left side, from which was slung a sword. (Nobility only.)

Gloves (imported from the Continent), worn only by the nobility and clergy of high rank.

11. COLOURS

Red, blue, green, pink, violet, purple and yellow. Gold and silver thread much used in embroidery.

An example of Saxon embroidery is the stole and maniple made for Bishop Fridestan, found in St. Cuthbert's coffin, and now in Durham Cathedral library.

WOMEN

1. THE TUNIC, or KIRTLE (see Glossary)

Worn over the smock (i.e. chemise), and put on over the head. Ground length, the hem sometimes embroidered. Sleeves long and close.

Materials. Linen for the wealthy.

Wool, often coarsely woven, for the poor.

2. THE SUPER-TUNIC, or ROC

Worn over the tunic by women of all classes, and put on over the head. A loose garment, ground length but frequently hitched up over the girdle exposing the tunic often up to knee level.

Generally lined with material of different colour (in tenth century).

Round neck usually hidden by veil draperies.

Sleeves

(1) Loose and cylindrical.

(2) Loose, broadening from shoulder to a wide bell-shaped opening below the elbow (tenth century).

Embroidered borders at neck, hem, sleeves, and very rarely a strip down the front.

Girdle. A wide sash, always the same colour as the gown, was essential.

3. THE MANTLE

Cut on the square, three-quarter to full length of the tunic, though usually hitched up in front. Fastened under the chin, probably by brooch or tie, the closure being hidden under the

3. 10TH CENTURY

(a) Super-tunic sleeve, with puckered and embroidered tunic sleeve emerging. Long veil. (b) Tunic with embroidered hem. Embroidered mantle. Long veil. Shoes.

drapery of the veil. Sometimes worn as a shawl, and usually lined with a contrasting colour (tenth century).

The DOUBLE MANTLE, identical with that worn by men.

4. HOSE or STOCKINGS
Presumably worn, but never seen.

5. FOOTWEAR
(1) SHOES, of the same shape as the men's.
    (*a*) With short centre slit over instep.
    (*b*) Open over foot, with short tongued upper (rare).
Colours. Usually black. Sometimes red, brown, orange or blue.
(2) CLOGS made of wood were worn.

6. HEADWEAR
THE VEIL OR HEAD-RAIL (synonymous terms) was indispensable; worn by all classes, even in bed, though sometimes discarded in intimate domestic life.

A queen's crown was worn over her veil.

It consisted of a long broad scarf, wide enough to reach from the forehead over the back of the head, so as to drape the shoulders, completely concealing the hair and leaving only the face visible. The long ends, passing over the shoulders, were crossed in front over the bosom and reached as low as the knees. It was draped in various ways, one end usually hanging free, the other tucked into the folds at the neck.

Materials. Fine or coarse, according to social position. Bright colours were common, matching or contrasting with the supertunic.

7. HAIR
Though concealed, there are on record 'golden hair ties and crispin needles to curl and plait the hair withal'.

8. ACCESSORIES
Jewellery
Head bands, circlets of gold, diadems and gold neckbands.

Rings, bracelets, ear-rings, beads and jewelled girdles are recorded though not depicted.

Examples (from Anglo-Saxon wills of the first half of the tenth century). 'Her best dun tunic . . . the better of her cloaks . . . her black tunics . . . her best holy veil . . . her best head band. . . .'

Note. Linen was expensive and used only by the rich (of both sexes).

Wool used by all.

Haircloth chiefly worn by the clergy.

Embroidery, known as 'English work', was celebrated throughout the Continent.

Eleventh Century

MEN

1. THE TUNIC

Fitting slightly closer to the body than the Saxon tunic, but widening to a full skirt. Put on over the head, with a low round neck or with a short slit down the front and fastened with a brooch.

Length

(a) Short, knee length. Worn by all classes.

(b) Long, ankle length. Chiefly worn by higher ranks on ceremonial occasions.

Sleeves. Moderately loose above, but narrowing to a good fit at the wrist.

Girdles, almost invariably worn, were narrow and often hidden, the short tunic being further shortened by being drawn up through the girdle and overhanging it.

The skirt of the short tunic sometimes slit up at the sides.

Decoration. Broad embroidered bands, woven or of appliqué work, round the neck, hem and wrists, and sometimes round the upper arm.

Materials with simple all-over designs were also used.

2. THE SUPER-TUNIC

Worn over the tunic. A loose garment put on over the head and made on a circular pattern.

Length. Either the same as that of the tunic or a little shorter, the lower border of the tunic being thus visible.

Sleeves. Loose, often expanding towards the wrists where they were sometimes turned back into a broad cuff. Also close fitting.

4. 11TH CENTURY

(a) Short super-tunic hitched up by girdle, showing tunic. Cloak. Leg bandages. Shoes. (b) Short tunic with side vents. Cloak clasped on right shoulder. (c) Long super-tunic over long tunic. Forked beard. (d) Short tunic with embroidered hem and band round upper arm. High class leg bandages arranged criss-cross.

Girdles. Optional, and used, as for the tunic, to hitch up and shorten the garment.

3. THE CLOAK

A loose wrap, rectangular or semicircular in cut; varied in length from knee to ankle. Fastened by tie or brooch, under the chin or on right shoulder; occasionally on the left.

Mantles of the nobility were of finer materials, often lined with fur, and usually long. Fastened by a cord threaded through attached metal rings sewn to opposite edges, a method only used by persons of rank.

Hooded cloaks were introduced at the end of the century, worn chiefly by travellers or rustics, and made of wool or skins.

4. LEGWEAR

(1) BREECHES OR BRAIES were loose trousers reaching to the ankle and fastened above by a threaded cord 'en coulisse' and tied well below waist level. The cord was sometimes made of leather, and usually emerged at intervals, the exposed portions serving in the twelfth century as points of attachment for long stockings, wallets, etc.

The legs of the breeches were:

(*a*) Fitted to the leg from knee to ankle, a style for the nobility.

(*b*) Loose fitting to the ankle and sometimes slit up behind for a variable distance; the type worn by the common people.

Both styles, but chiefly the loose variety, were made to fit the leg more closely by means of stockings drawn on over the breeches up to the knee, or by means of leg bandages.

(2) LEG BANDAGES were strips of linen or wool, bound spirally (or by the higher ranks in a criss-cross pattern) from foot or ankle to below the knee over the trouser leg or stockings. Ceased to be fashionable after 1100, though worn later occasionally by rustics, but reappeared in the thirteenth century for a short period as a fashion for the nobility and then bound criss-cross and reaching above the knees.

(3) STOCKINGS (hose or chausses) were of wool or linen, cut

5. 11TH CENTURY

(a) A Norman hair style. (b and c) 'Phrygian bonnets' or caps.
(d) Stockings with ornamental tops. Socks. Shoes. (e) Shoe showing
leather thongs. (f) Stockings with ornamental tops. Shoes.

23

to the shape of the leg. (Knitting, as a craft, was unknown in England until the second half of the sixteenth century.) They reached to just below the knee, very rarely above, often ending with an ornamental border which may have served as a garter. Sometimes instead of having a foot the stocking ended in a stirrup.

5. FOOTWEAR

(1) SHOES were pointed and shaped to the foot, distinguishing right from left. No raised heels. Usually of leather, with decorative patterns on the shoes of the nobility.

Forms

(*a*) Closed to the ankle with a short tongue over the instep.

(*b*) Slit down over the instep and fastened with an ankle thong.

(2) BOOTS. Short and fastened with thongs, were uncommon in the eleventh century.

6. HEADWEAR

(1) BARE-HEADED, which was fashionable through the eleventh, twelfth and thirteenth centuries.

(2) THE HOOD attached to the cloak.

(3) THE SAXON 'PHRYGIAN CAP', with a liking for the straight pointed variety.

7. HAIR

Up to 1087.

The older men wore their hair medium long to nape of neck, with centre parting or shaggy fringe. Beards often forked and moustaches of medium length. Moustache alone extremely rare, but beards without moustaches quite common, the face being clean shaven round the mouth. The younger men were clean-shaven. Their hair was brushed back from the forehead with or without a centre parting, and fell to the neck or shoulders. Some Norman youths had short hair which was shaved at the back of the head. This was a limited fashion supposed to originate from Aquitaine.

Later. 1087 to 1150, but moderated from 1100 to 1125, all men, young and old, allowed their hair and beards to grow as long as possible, some curling, crimping and plaiting them.

8. ACCESSORIES

The *Girdle* was a plain band or cord.

Gloves were almost unknown.

Aprons were worn by the lower classes.

Swords were not worn by civilians throughout the Middle Ages, being a badge of knighthood.

Eleventh Century

WOMEN

1. THE GOWN or KIRTLE

Corresponding to the masculine Tunic, but always long, more or less ground length. Worn over the smock (chemise), it was loose, cut like the male tunic, and always worn with a girdle.

Sleeves. Close fitting, and tight at the wrist.

2. THE SUPER-TUNIC or ROC

A long loose garment worn over the Kirtle, probably for warmth; similar in design to the male super-tunic.

Sleeves. Loose, expanding to a wide opening at the wrist, though occasionally moderately close fitting.

Some were tubular and extended well beyond the hand acting as a muff.

3. THE CLOAK or MANTLE

Similar to the male garment, but almost invariably of ground length. Tied in front, often quite loosely by cords.

Cloaks were not hooded for women.

Double Mantles still worn.

4. LEGWEAR

No braies or drawers were worn by women (in fact, not until the nineteenth century).

Stockings or Hose, of cloth, similar to the men's but sometimes reaching above the knees; kept up by ties.

6. 11TH CENTURY

(a) Super-tunic, hitched up by girdle, showing kirtle. Double mantle.
Veil. (b) Long-sleeved super-tunic. Veil. (c) Mantle. Super-tunic.
Kirtle. Veil.

5. FOOTWEAR

Shoes similar to those worn by men.

6. HEADWEAR

THE VEIL, Coverchief or Kerchief (French—couvre-chef), corresponding to the Saxon head-rail (from antiquity to the end of the Middle Ages), but smaller, was rectangular or part of a circle. One straight edge hung over the forehead, concealing the hair; the rest falling in draperies round the face and neck, and often crossed over in front, thus encircling the face.

7. HAIR

Flowing loose and uncovered was a mode only allowed for young girls. Otherwise it was concealed.

ACCESSORIES
As for the tenth century.

Twelfth Century

MEN

1. THE TUNIC

As in the eleventh century, but new variations appeared.

(*a*) With close fitting body, and long skirt generally slit up in front to thigh level, and worn with a girdle to carry the sword.

Sleeves fairly close fitting with a sudden bell-shaped expansion at the wrist, or with the lower portion hanging to form a pendulous cuff which might be rolled up for action.

Use limited to the nobility [1130s to 1170s].

(Compare with the more exaggerated form worn by women.)

(*b*) Short, with loose tubular sleeves often rolled back at the wrist.

Worn by peasants and social inferiors.

(*c*) Cut in a style characteristic of the thirteenth century, with Magyar sleeves, and the front of the skirt cut up to the girdle (End of twelfth century to 1300).

New Neck Line, in which the front slit might be:

(1) Diagonal from neck across the chest, or

(2) Horizontal from neck to shoulder.

These new neck lines appeared in any tunic from the end of the twelfth to early fourteenth centuries, but were uncommon.

2. THE SUPER-TUNIC

Similar to that of the eleventh century. A girdle was optional. Occasionally worn alone, with a girdle, but not worn with tunics of style (*a*).

28

7. 12TH CENTURY

(a) Tunic with pendulous cuffs; slit skirt showing long stockings,
probably soled hose (p.31) drawn up over braies. (*c.* 1165.) (b) Ceremonial mantle. Embroidered super-tunic with pendulous cuffs. Long
tunic. Embroidered ankle strap shoes. Note hair style. (1130–70).
(c) Cloak fastened by knotting. (1140–60). (d) Rustic with short
hooded cloak, short tunic with loose rolled up sleeves. Short decorated
boots. Long beard. (*c.* 1140). (e) Fur-lined cloak, jewelled clasp on
right shoulder. Super-tunic with wide elbow sleeves. Soled hose. Hair
style of young man. Small hat with knob. (*c.* 1170–80).

8. 12TH CENTURY

(a) Jewelled glove. (b) Purse. (c) Leg bandages of rustic. (d) Long boots.
(e) Short stockings, slipping down. Ankle shoes. (f) Short stockings.
High shoes. (g) Striped stockings. Short boots. (h) and (i) varying shoe
styles.

30

Sleeves. (*a*) With pendulous cuffs; uncommon.

(*b*) Loose, and often elbow-length only.

Pelisson is a super-tunic lined with fur (Came in *c.* 1165).

3. THE CLOAK and MANTLE

As in the eleventh century. A new variety was a very small cloak lined with fur.

Common method of fastening: The upper corner of the neck edge on one side was pulled through a ring sewn to the opposite corner, and then knotted to keep it in position. Otherwise ornamental clasp or brooch used.

Materials. Mantles for the nobility of rich materials frequently lined with fur.

Cloaks for rustics usually hooded and often made of skins worn with the hairy surface outside.

4. LEGWEAR

(1) BREECHES, similar to those of the eleventh century continued for the first half of the twelfth. They then became shortened to the knee, becoming braies or drawers (i.e. undergarments) in the second half of the century, and were chiefly made of linen.

(2) STOCKINGS

(*a*) Short, ending below the knee often with an ornamental border.

(*b*) Long, reaching to mid-thigh, and shaped to fit the leg, widening above the knee so that they could be pulled up over the braies. They usually ended in a pointed tongue in front from which a tie attached the stocking to the breech girdle at a point of emergence from the coulisse.

Some hose had stirrups without feet; others had no feet.

Footed hose with a thin leather sole attached (Saxon, then 1160s to end of fifteenth century), were worn without shoes, and were made of stout woollen material or even of thin leather. (King John had a pair of cowhide.)

Colours were bright, and stripes were popular.

The finer qualities were very costly.

9. 12TH CENTURY

(a) Small round cap with stalk. (a) and (b) Tunics (old style). Cloaks. Long stockings and long boots. (1121-48). (c) Coif. Hood thrown back. (Late 12th c.). (d) Tunic with 'magyar' sleeves. 'Phrygian' cap. Long stockings. Short pointed boots. (Late 12th c.). (e) Cloak clasped on left shoulder. (f) Hooded cloak. (g) Large hat. (c. 1121-48.)

32

5. FOOTWEAR

Boots and shoes worn by all classes.

(1) SHOES

(*a*) Open over the foot and fastened in front of the ankle with a strap secured by brooch or buckle. For the wealthy these shoes had ornamental bands or decorative designs over the foot or round the heel.

(*b*) High round the ankle and slit down the sides or in front. Sometimes laced up.

(*c*) Shoes with short uppers but cut high behind the heel began to appear (end of twelfth century).

(2) BOOTS

(*a*) Reaching to mid calf or knee; laced on the inner side or down the centre; often with brightly coloured turn-over tops.

(*b*) Short, reaching just above the ankle.

Shaped as in the eleventh century, but often more pointed. (The long-pointed shoes described in contemporary writings as of exaggerated length are not, however, seen in illustrations of the time.)

Materials for footwear: Leather (cowhide or oxhide), cloth, fish-skin, and sometimes silk.

6. HEADWEAR

(1) THE HOOD, as a separate entity [1160 to 1460] was the most characteristic covering; a loose pointed cowl with attached cape reaching the shoulders.

The *cape,* known as the *gorget,* was usually closed all round, so that the hood had to be put on over the head. When open in front (far less usual form) it was fastened at the neck by brooch or clasp.

(2) THE POINTED PHRYGIAN CAP. (Tenth to end of twelfth century, and unfashionably into the thirteenth.)

(3) SMALL ROUND CAP with a stalk; or with a rolled brim and with or without a stalk.

(4) A STALKED SOFT CAP, resembling a beret.

(5) HATS with large brims and low crowns were worn by travellers, and frequently over the hood. Usually there were two

strings which when loosely tied under the chin enabled the hat to be thrown back on to the neck without falling off.

(6) SMALL HAT with round crown and turned-down brim, decorated with a knob instead of a stalk.

(7) THE COIF (end of twelfth century to 1440, after which used by professions). A close fitting plain linen bonnet (resembling a baby's bonnet) which covered the ears and confined the hair; tied under the chin. Worn either alone or under any other type of headgear.

Gold or silver *fillets,* often jewelled, were worn by nobles.

7. HAIR

Long hair to the shoulders and long beards and moustaches were usual. The hair was often parted on either side of the head, the central portion being brought forward in a shaggy fringe over the forehead. These styles were slightly shorter all round, for a few years at the beginning and the end of the twelfth century. (The moustache without a beard was never an English fashion in the Middle Ages.)

Young men were often clean shaven, with the back hair to the nape of the neck only.

8. ACCESSORIES

The Girdle became more ornamental about 1150, and was tied like a sash in front with hanging ends [1170–90]; or, long and elaborate, was fastened with ornamental buckles [1175]. The purse was often attached to one hanging end.

Wallets or Pouches, varying in size from purses to 'handbags', varied also in shape and decoration; slung from either (a) the girdle, or (b) the breech girdle (also called the brayer); they were in the latter case hidden under the tunic.

Keys were usually slung from the brayer and so concealed.

Gloves only worn by men of rank, and then seldom. Gloves with jewelled backs were worn by kings, as shown by the effigies of Henry II and Richard I at Fontevraud.

Not before the thirteenth century were gloves worn generally in England.

Walking Sticks, plain or decorated, were rare.

Jewellery. Rings, brooches, buckles, clasps and ornamental fillets of gold or silver were worn by nobles.

Decoration of Garments. Embroidery continued to be fashionable.

Dagging (*c.* 1170–1500, but the height of fashion from 1380–1440), a crude form of vandyking, was used at this period for the lower edge of the hood gorget and sometimes round the bottom of tunic or super-tunic.

Materials. Leather, often with the hair left on and with that surface outside, was used by peasants for tunics and mantles.

Wool, linen and silk were also in use.

Twelfth Century

WOMEN

1. THE KIRTLE or GOWN

Worn over the smock, and corresponding to the male tunic, as in the previous century, and always with a girdle.

Sleeves plain and close fitting at first.

The new style [1130s–1170], appearing after the first quarter, was characteristic of the twelfth century, but worn by ladies of rank only. The bodice was moulded to the figure, fitting tightly down to the hips; below that level the skirt, cut to expand considerably, fell in many close folds to the ground, often spreading behind into a train. The bodice was frequently depicted with an all-over pattern suggestive of smocking; its method of fastening is uncertain; sometimes it seems to have been laced up, either in front or at the back. The round neck without decolletage, and the skin-tight fit, would make it impossible to put on the garment over the head. Occasionally the neckline was cut in a moderate V in front, especially with noble ladies, thus exposing the top of the smock.

The *sleeves* were tight fitting to below the elbows, where they abruptly expanded into long hanging cuffs often reaching the ground and appearing like 'streamers' dependent from the wrists. Sometimes these were bulged out below forming pouches. The streamers, and the skirt draperies, might be tied into knots to keep them out of the way.

The sleeves were sometimes of a different colour from that of the gown, green being popular.

2. THE GIRDLE

Extremely long and decorative, was either a thick cord of silk,

10. 12TH CENTURY

(a) Kirtle with pendant cuffs. Girdle tied in method (b) (p. 38). Mantle. Hair in two plaits. Veil encircled with gold fillet. (1140–50.) (b) Kirtle with pendulous cuffs. Girdle tied in method (a) (p. 38). Mantle fastened with brooch. Crown over veil. (1140–60). (c) Super-tunic with pendant cuffs. No girdle. Veil, bound with knotted band. (1130–70). (d) Hooded cloak. Kirtle with pendant and pouched cuffs. Gloves, unfingered, with long streamers. (c. 1150). (e) Super-tunic with pendant cuffs. Hair in fouriaux (p. 40). (1130–50).

wool or linen, or was made of thongs plaited together or worked into a design on a broader belt ending in silk cords.

Methods of wearing:

(*a*) Passed round the hips to be tied at a lower level in front, the ends hanging down in midline almost to the ankles.

(*b*) Passed round the front of the waist and knotted or crossed over in the small of the back, then brought forward and downward and tied in front, the ends hanging in midline to the ankles.

N.B. The exaggerations of this style diminished during the second half of the century.

3. THE SUPER-TUNIC

Followed the pattern of the previous century, but was closer fitting, with a tendency to exaggerated length, drapery effects, and wider sleeves, which sometimes had pendent cuffs and could not be worn over a gown with similar sleeves.

Pelissons were worn by ladies of rank.

4. THE CLOAK and MANTLE

Similar to that of the eleventh century.

Hooded cloaks, probably for winter, were in common use towards the close of the century.

5. LEGWEAR

Stockings, gartered by woollen ties above or below the knees, continued in use.

6. FOOTWEAR

Shoes, as in the eleventh century.

7. HEADWEAR

(1) THE VEIL. As formerly; noble ladies always wore veils in public during the first half of the century.

(2) HALF BENDS (Bands) of gold, or complete circles such as

a

b

c

11. 12TH CENTURY

(a) Veil, with fillet and wimple. (b) and (c) Decorated shoes (late 12th c.).

diadems, were worn over the veil, helping to keep it in place. Queen's crowns were worn over the veil.

(3) A LONG NARROW BAND, passed round the head over the veil and knotted on one side, leaving long flowing ends, was sometimes worn during this period (*c.* 1130s–1170s) when streamers were fashionable.

(4) BARBETTE AND FILLET (late twelfth century to early fourteenth) consisted of a linen band passed under the chin to the temples, worn with a linen 'crown' encircling the head (see thirteenth century).

(5) THE WIMPLE OR GORGET (1150–1340, after which unfashionable, and in fifteenth century worn by widows only). Made of fine white linen or silk, was a neck covering draped over the bosom (often tucked inside the neck of the gown), and round the front of the neck; the ends, then drawn up to frame the face, were pinned to the hair above the ears or on top of the head under the veil which was usually worn as well. Sometimes the wimple completely covered the head.

8. HAIR

Mostly concealed by veil and wimple or veil alone, the latter being the usual mode for all except the nobility. Young girls wore their hair uncovered, with a centre parting, the locks falling loose or curled on to the shoulders; or with one or two long pigtails, plaited or enclosed in a silk sheath (*'fouriau'*). This is usually depicted coloured white with red circular stripes.

New style for those of very high rank [1120–1150]. The hair, parted in the middle, was then braided into two long tresses which descended in front of the shoulders reaching sometimes to below the knees. The plaits were reinforced by false hair or tow and braided with ribbon, and the ends often tipped with ornaments. Or the plaits were encased in silk fouriaux. This style was usually worn with a loose flowing veil secured by a gold circlet or, in the case of a queen, by a crown.

9. ACCESSORIES

Elegant *Girdles,* as described.

Jewellery. Ornamental chaplets of gold, bracelets, rings, necklaces and brooches.

Gloves rare, but occasionally worn by ladies of rank. Even gloves might have streamer-like cuffs, as depicted on a lady with birds. In this case the gloves had thumbs but no separate compartments for the fingers (Cotton MS. Nero CIV).

N.B. *Rouge* was in general use by the higher ranks.

Thirteenth Century

MEN

1. TUNIC or COTE

In addition to the former styles of short and long tunics, worn with a girdle, a new cut appeared, characteristic of this century. The *sleeves* were made in one piece with the body (as in magyar sleeves) leaving a wide armhole often extending to the waist; the sleeve being cut to slope off to a narrow tight cuff at the wrist. (End of twelfth century to end of thirteenth century.)

Both long and short tunics were now usually slit up in front as far as the girdle.

2. SUPER-TUNIC or SURCOTE (a term chiefly belonging to the thirteenth century). Continued to be worn by the less fashionable, a girdle being optional.

New Styles

(1) TABARD variety, without sleeves. Consisted of a panel front and back, expanding downwards from the shoulders to reach calf level or lower. It was put on over the head, having a wide neck aperture, the open sides being sewn together from just below the waist, or fastened with clasps. It was also often slit up in front to the same level. No belt worn.

(2) The GARDE-CORPS, (thirteenth and early fourteenth century) was a voluminous garment hanging in folds to the ankles or just below the knees. Made with wide tubular sleeves gathered at the shoulders and reaching well beyond the hands. For convenience the arm could be passed through a long vertical slit in the front of the upper part of the sleeve, which was left hanging

12. 13TH CENTURY

(a) Sleeveless surcoat showing tunic below. Coif on head. (Late 13th c.)
(b) Garde-corps. (Mid 13th c.) (c) Embroidered sleeveless surcoat with
front slit to skirt. Tunic with embroidered arm bands. Stalked round
cap. Ankle strap shoes. (Mid 13th c.) (d) Long tunic with 'magyar'
sleeves and front slit to skirt. Mantle with jewelled clasp. Criss-cross
leg bandages reaching above knees (high class) over soled hose.
Stalked cap and long embroidered gloves. (Early 13th c.)

43

loose. This super-tunic was generally hooded and put on over the head.

Usually no belt was worn with it.

(3) A LOOSE SUPER-TUNIC, with short wide sleeves reaching just below the elbows, was occasionally worn. A belt, often buckled, was optional [1260–1360].

(4) The GARNACHE [1260–1400], reaching below the knees, was made like the Tabard type, but with shoulder line cut wide enough for the material to fall down to the elbows on each side, producing cape-like sleeves. With long loose sleeves, worn off and on in 14th century.

The sides were either
(a) Joined just below waist level.
(b) Sewn up from waist to hem.
(c) Left open all down the sides.
No belt worn.

3. FITCHETS (First appeared c. 1250)

Vertical slits resembling pocket openings made in the super-tunics which had no side openings. Through them the purse or keys, slung from the girdle of the tunic, could be reached.

4. CLOAKS and MANTLES

Unchanged.

5. LEG WEAR

(1) STOCKINGS unchanged. Sometimes gartered below the knee with narrow strips of material.

(2) LEG BANDAGES for the nobility, with a criss-cross arrangement, reaching above the knees were worn for a short period. (c. 1200)

6. FOOTWEAR

(1) SHOES, shaped to the foot.
(a) Plain, and mostly closed round ankle, with inner lacing, or sometimes buckled.
(b) Open over foot and cut high behind the ankle, as in twelfth century to end of thirteenth century.

13. 13TH CENTURY HEADWEAR

(a) Small hat with knob on crown. (b) Hat with round crown and rolled brim. Also shows short sleeve of super-tunic. (c) Coif. (d) Hat slung on shoulders. (e) Hat worn over coif.

a

b

c

d

e

f

14. 13TH CENTURY

(a) (b) (c). Peasants in tunics and straw hats over coifs in (a) and (c).
(d) Short boots. (e) Two purses. (f) Glove with embroidered back.

(*c*) Open over foot and closed by ankle or instep strap.

(2) BOOTS, or Buskins. Coloured tops for a brief period. All now had a much looser fit. Many barely reached the calf.

7. HEADWEAR

(1) THE HOOD, as in previous century.

(2) THE STALKED ROUND CAP or Beret, as in eleventh century.

(3) THE LARGE BRIMMED TRAVELLING HAT, as in eleventh century.

(4) HAT WITH BROAD BRIM turned up at the back; occasionally worn reversed with turn-up in front.

(5) HAT WITH ROUND CROWN, sometimes with a knob on the crown, and a moderate brim with a downward slope; or a rolled brim or a hat like a small bowler.

(6) THE COIF (end of twelfth century to 1440) continued in use and was much in evidence.

8. HAIR

Worn with centre parting or a fringe, and waved to nape of the neck. Beard and moustache of moderate length only, as compared to previous century. Young men had 'bobbed' hair with straight or waved fringe, or a roll curl across the forehead. A similar curl was sometimes worn at the nape of the neck, and this always escaped from the coif if worn. The face was clean-shaven in young men.

9. ACCESSORIES

As in the twelfth century.

Gloves, worn by the highest rank, were either long, reaching nearly to the elbows, or wrist length.

These were often decorated with a broad strip of gold embroidery down the back as far as the knuckles. (Edward I was buried with jewelled gloves). Individual glove makers are mentioned in Colchester records in 1295.

Gloves began to be more widely worn towards the end of the century.

Buttons, gilded or silver, were used as ornaments.

Thirteenth Century

WOMEN

1. THE KIRTLE or GOWN (also called Cote).

Worn with a girdle, and similar to the simple garment of the twelfth century, but the neckline tended to be slightly lower; or it was made with a short V opening which was closed at the throat with a brooch. These gowns remained very long with full draperies and trains.

Sleeves, fitting or loose. The tight sleeves were sometimes laced.

Fitchets (appeared first *c.* 1250), as in the male garment, were made in the woman's kirtle at the end of this century, implying that sometimes the purse was slung from a sash round the smock.

2. THE SURCOAT

(*a*) A voluminous garment with long massive draperies. Put on over the head through a wide neck opening. The sleeves, ending between elbow and wrist, expanded to a wide aperture (first half of thirteenth century). Subsequently they were closer fitting.

No girdle worn as a rule.

(*b*) The sleeveless surcoat, similar but without sleeves, the armhole consisting of a long vertical slit. The neck opening was wide from side to side, producing the effect of shoulder straps.

No girdle worn.

3. THE PELISSON

A super-tunic lined with fur, as previously worn.

15. 13TH CENTURY

(a) Surcoat (embroidered) with kirtle sleeve emerging. Crown over
veil. Mantle. (b) Fur-lined mantle over kirtle with girdle. Veil worn
open. (Late 13th c.) (c) Trained kirtle with typical 13th century sleeves.
Gold circlet and loose hair of young girl.

Furs. Fox and squirrel were the fashionable kinds; the commoner sorts were rabbit, cat and hare.

4. CLOAKS and MANTLES

Very long, and often trained, as in twelfth century.

Occasionally hooded, for travelling, and used to end of fourteenth century.

Mantles for the higher ranks were made of silk lined with fur. These were sometimes used as *dressing gowns,* e.g. Henry III gave his sister Isabel 'two scarlet cloaks, one lined with fur, the other with silk, to be used when she rose at night'.

5. STOCKINGS

As in the twelfth century.

Henry III ordered three yards of bruneta cloth worked with gold to make stockings for his sister.

6. FOOTWEAR

Shoes, as for men.

7. HEADWEAR

(1) THE VEIL, as in previous century.

(2) THE BARBETTE AND FILLET. Typical of the thirteenth and early fourteenth centuries. Worn without the veil.

The barbette was a linen band passed under the chin and pinned on the top of the head. It often broadened considerably at the angle of the jaw, sometimes giving it a coif-like appearance.

The fillet was a stiffened linen circlet varying in width from a narrow band to a broad crown with a slight outward splay. *Goffered Fillets* were common [*c.* 1250] though this decoration was used earlier.

Gold circlets or coronets were worn inside the fillet by noble ladies.

The shape of the fillet changed to accommodate itself to the changing hair styles, and later became broadened from side to side, instead of being circular.

16. 13TH CENTURY

Surcoat with fairly close sleeves and kirtle sleeves to wrist. Mantle
much draped and cord hanging loose in front. Wimple, veil and fillet.
(c. 1269).

51

17. 13TH CENTURY HEADWEAR

(a) (b) (c) (d) (e) Various types of barbette and fillet headdress (p. 50).
(f) Veil and wimple. (g) Wimple alone, pinned up at the sides. (Also
early 14th c.)

The hair was turned up at the neck and pinned to the barbette, or enclosed in a net or *crespine*. This hair net confined the hair under the barbette and fillet, and was never worn alone except by women of the lower class.

Garlands or *chaplets* of flowers or of goldsmith's work were worn by young girls.

(3)   *The Wimple* continued to be worn; this with the veil, or the veil alone, might be worn with a fillet.

Veils and wimples were sometimes dyed yellow at the end of the century.

> *Wymples, kerchyves, saffrund betyde*
> *Yellugh under yellugh they hyde.*
>
> (Robert of Brunnes *Handlyng Synne,* 1303)

8. HAIR

Almost invisible throughout this century.

(*a*) Turned back from the forehead and twisted or plaited into a roll at the back of the head, and covered with the crespine.

(*b*) Later [1270] from a centre parting it was rolled or plaited on each side of the face over the ears, and above these side plaits, which were usually covered by the crespine, the widened fillet was fitted.

9. ACCESSORIES

Gloves, of fine linen, were worn by ladies of high rank to protect their hands from sun-burn.

Jewellery. Gold chaplets, bracelets, rings, necklaces and ornamental buttons.

When Queen Eleanor attended her sister's wedding in 1290, she wore a dress 'renovated for the occasion and adorned with 636 silver buttons'. (*The Wardrobe and Household of Henry, son of Edward I.* Hilda Johnstone.)

18. 13TH CENTURY HEADWEAR
(a) Coronet over hair plaited over ears and twisted up behind. (b) Barbette and goffered fillet.

First Half of
the Fourteenth Century

MEN

The styles of the late thirteenth century persisted through the first half of the fourteenth, and, unfashionably, until near the end.

During the *first quarter,* long ceremonial garments, e.g. tunics and super-tunics, were retained.

During the *second quarter* a break from the traditions of the past became noticeable, with fashion moving towards better cut and producing garments of closer fit revealing the shape of the body. At the same time men's clothes became steadily shorter, exposing the legs in long tight-fitting hose.

Buttons, hitherto mainly decorative, came to be widely used as practical fastenings though preserving an ornamental character in gold, silver, brass, copper, crystal, glass, as well as silk, damask and hair.[1]

1. THE SHORT TUNIC

This, sometimes slit up in front and with sleeves of the magyar (for a few years) or plain form, continued in use by the lower classes. It was worn with a girdle, and sometimes shortened to hip level revealing the braies; but the tunic was rapidly going out of fashion, being superseded by

2. THE GIPON, POURPOINT or DOUBLET (replacing the tunic) 1335.

The name 'doublet', though used in France at this period, did

[1] Mrs. Russell-Smith has found evidence that buttons were used as fastenings in the 13th century and even by the Romans.

19. 14TH CENTURY, 1ST HALF

(a) Peasant's tunic with front slit to skirt, showing long stockings with
button fastening, also garter. Ankle shoes. (b) Gipon, and ankle strap
shoes. (c) Gipon buttoned all down front, hood thrown back. (d)
Gipon worn with belt, open below. Hood with short liripipe. Garters
and decorated shoes.

not become a general term for the civilian garment in England until the fifteenth century.

The Gipon, replacing the tunic, was worn over the shirt, being a close-fitting, slightly waisted garment, falling without folds or gathers to just above the knees. Its bodice was padded, usually throughout.

Fastened all down the front by lacing or a close row of ball or flat buttons [1335]. With the less fashionable, buttoned to waist only.

The *neck* was low and round [1335–1420].

Sleeves tight to the wrist, the fit obtained by a row of buttons matching the rest, from elbow downwards.

> Botones azur' d wor ilke ane
> From his elboth to his hand.

(From a MS. poem (Cotton Julius).)

A *girdle* was rare, as the gipon was usually covered and the belt confined to the cote-hardie. During the second half of the century, however, when the gipon was frequently worn without the cote-hardie, then a belt was essential.

3. OVER-GARMENTS

(1) The COTE-HARDIE of the gentry [1330–1450].

This replaced the super-tunic and was worn over the gipon. It was low-necked and tight-fitting, buttoned or laced down the front to waist level whence it flared into a full skirt open in front and reaching to the knees.

The *sleeves,* ending at the bend of the elbow in front, expanded abruptly behind into a short tongue-shaped hanging flap, varying in length and breadth.

Its *girdle* or belt was usually worn below waist level.

(2) The COTE-HARDIE of the lower classes was looser and frequently without front fastening; put on over the head through a wide opening which was often then narrowed by folding over the material in front and presumably pinning it.

The *skirt,* ankle or knee length, was generally slit up the front to the girdle or short of it.

The *sleeves* resembled those of the more fashionable garment.

20. 14TH CENTURY, 1ST HALF

(a) Cote-hardie with exaggerated sleeve flaps. Hood with liripipe. Ankle shoes. (b) Long cote-hardie, showing buttoned gipon sleeves. Fur-lined mantle. Decorated ankle shoes. (c) Garnache with tongue-shaped lapels, over old-fashioned super-tunic and tunic. Large country hat with strings, worn over hood. Large loose buskins. (d) Cote-hardie taken of over the head. Old-fashioned tunic.

21. 14TH CENTURY, 1ST HALF

(a) Hood with liripipe twisted round head. Short tunic. Thigh length boots, buckled below calf. (b) (c) (d) Garnaches. (e) Peasant in short tunic showing braies. (f) (g) Peasants in hoods, shoulder capes and short boots.

The *girdle* or belt worn (*a*) at waist level;

(*b*) at the fashionable level;

(*c*) not worn. With this style fitchets were frequent.

(3) THE GARNACHE continued as in the latter part of the thirteenth century, the length reaching to mid-calf or ankle. The neck opening had a feature characteristic of the fourteenth century, namely two small *tongue-shaped lapels* at the neck of a paler shade than the garment itself and sometimes furred.

(4) THE GARDE-CORPS continued for a few years.

(5) The loose short-sleeved, or sometimes sleeveless, SUPER-TUNIC persisted, the latter sometimes slit up in front from hem to thighs.

(6) THE TABARD style had become rare.

(7) MANTLES were, as previously, long ceremonial garments.

4. OUTER GARMENTS

(1) THE CLOAK, usually long, circular in cut, was fastened in front or buttoned on the right shoulder. Costly linings were fashionable among the nobility.

(2) SHOULDER CAPES [1330–1430] independent of hoods, were worn.

(3) CAPES WITH LOW COLLARS, cut on the circle, reaching to mid-thigh and closely buttoned down the front. Some had hoods.

5. LEGWEAR

HOSE OR STOCKINGS

(*a*) Knee length, ending just below the joint.

(*b*) Thigh length, reaching well above the knee.

(*c*) Socks reaching to just below the calf; all frequently decorated with circular bands e.g. red and white [*c.* 1340].

Soled hose, i.e. with a thin leather sole attached and worn without shoes or boots, continued in use to the end of the fifteenth century.

Decoration of hose. Often of different colours from the main garment, or different from each other; or one leg might be

22. 14TH CENTURY, 1ST HALF
FOOTWEAR

(a) (b) (d) Ankle strap shoes. (c) Soled hose with circular stripes
(*c.* 1315). (e) (f) Ankle fitting shoes with outer and inner lacing.

divided vertically into two different colours. This arose from the widespread custom, all through the fourteenth century, of nobles having garments embroidered with heraldic motifs, producing parti-coloured effects from the mixed colour schemes.

Garters. Strips of wool or linen, often embroidered, tied below the knee, the ends tucked in or left dangling, used for long or short stockings.

Long stockings were sometimes also attached by being buttoned in front of the thighs, possibly to a string from the braie girdle.

6. FOOTWEAR

(1) SHOES

(*a*) Well cut and shaped to the foot with a point at the big toe; fitting round the ankle and laced on the inner or sometimes the outer side.

(*b*) Cut away over instep (like a slipper) and fastened round ankle by strap and buckle.

In the higher ranks shoes were decorated by being embroidered or punched into patterns (squares, dots or flowers).

(2) BOOTS or BUSKINS

For riding some were shaped up to the thighs and fastened by buttons, laces or buckles below the calf; others were loose and unshaped, made to fit the leg by means of a front fold which was buttoned or hooked down the outside of the calf. For walking, *short boots* ending below the calf and buttoned or laced on the inner or occasionally outer side were commonly used.

'To Robert le Fermar, bootmaker of Flete Street, per six pair of boots with tassels of silk and drops of silver-gilt, price of each pair, five shillings, bought for the King's use. Westminster, 24 May. £1 10s.' From Wardrobe Accounts of Edward II in 1311.

7. HEADWEAR

(1) THE HOOD continued in use, but developed a *liripipe,* i.e. an extension of the point of the cowl into a hanging tail. The liripipe (1330 to 1450 and on hats to 1480) was long or short, and (with rare exceptions) was always made in one piece with the

23. 14TH CENTURY, 1ST HALF

(a) Ceremonial fur-lined mantle over long embroidered super-tunic. Embroidered ankle strap shoes. Crown worn over coif. Hawking glove. (c. 1325). (b) Man in hood worn turban-wise (p. 65 example (d)) putting on long stockings. (c. 1340.) (c) Hat worn over hood with short liripipe. (c. 1340.)

24. 14TH CENTURY, 1ST HALF
HEADWEAR

(a) and (c) Hats with brims peaked in front, turned up behind. (b) Stalked round cap. (d) Stalked 'beret'. (e) Large travelling hat with fastening cord, worn over hood.

hood. If cut vertically it would hang on one side or the other; if cut horizontally it would hang down the back. The long liripipe would often be twisted round the head turban-wise. The liripipe was very rarely lined.

Materials for hoods. Generally cloth lined with same material; sometimes with fur; rarely with taffeta.

The lining was sometimes of a different colour from the hood; sometimes this distinction was given only to the face piece.

An embroidered band round the lower border of the gorget was common.

(2) HATS

(*a*) Thirteenth century styles continued, mainly worn by country folk, the stalked beret being very common.

(*b*) A hat with a small round or domed crown, the wide brim turned up sharply behind and forming a peak in front.

(*c*) A high domed crown or round 'bowler' shape, either having a rolled or close turned-up brim (1325 to end of fifteenth century).

(*d*) A turban headgear made from the hood. The face opening was drawn over the head and turned up into a rolled brim, leaving the point of the hood and gorget to flop over on opposite sides. This became the fashionable 'hood turban' of the next period [1340–1380].

(3) THE COIF continued to be worn.

8. HAIR

Styles of the thirteenth century continued in fashion, with a clean-shaven face, though sometimes beards with or without moustaches but without side whiskers, were worn, e.g. 'these bearded bucks' (Robert of Brunne). The roll curl across the forehead and at the nape of the neck, with a clean shaven-face, was very prevalent.

9. ACCESSORIES

The *Girdle* or Belt became very ornamental, often being tied in front or buckled, the long ends hanging loose.

25. 14TH CENTURY, 1ST HALF
HEADWEAR

(a) (c) (d) Hoods worn turban-wise with facial opening fitting the head (p. 65 example (d)). (b) (f) Hoods with long liripipes (b) also shows cote-hardie and hawking glove. (e) (h) Hats with round crowns and (e) close turn-up brim, (h) rolled brim. (g) High hats with domed crowns and rolled brims, worn over hoods.

26. 14TH CENTURY, 1ST HALF

(a) Tunic, close fitting, verging towards gipon, with pouch and dagger
at belt. Hood slung over shoulder. (b) Garnache and hawking gloves.
(c) Peasants' gloves. (d) (e) Peasant with hood, tunic, (d) glove tucked
in belt, socks with circular stripes, garter.

The *Dagger* was slung vertically from the belt on one side, or suspended from a cord tied to the belt, or fastened to the back of the pouch.

The *Pouch* was also slung from the belt, and carried by all classes.

The *Penner* and *Inkhorn* were similarly slung from the belt.

Gloves, all made with a spreading gauntlet cuff, were universally worn, often merely carried in the hand, by all classes. Those worn by nobility were embroidered, by labourers often had separate thumb and first finger, the other three fingers being in one compartment. Made of coarse thick materials. 'The glovers of London were recognised as a separate organisation circa 1349' (Linthicum).

Aprons were worn by servants.

First Half of Fourteenth Century

WOMEN

1. THE KIRTLE or GOWN

Continued at first unaltered.

But by 1330 this, with the Cote-hardie, had changed fundamentally. Instead of concealing the shape of the body it revealed the feminine contours, being cut to mould the figure to the hips, whence it expanded abruptly and fell in widening folds to the ground.

The neck was low, sometimes baring the shoulders, a startling innovation to some contemporaries. 'A gown open thus at the neck seems like the hole of a privy' (From MS. of 1300 to 1310).

The sleeves were tight and long, either buttoned from elbow to wrist or sewn up. 'To render her vesture more perfect a silver needle was filled with a thread of gold, and both her sleeves were closely sewed' (*'Roman de la Rose'*).

The kirtle was *fastened* by front or back lacing from neck to waist, or just below.

The girdle, (optional) was worn round the hips and might be exposed to view through the side openings of the sleeveless surcoat.

2. OVER GARMENTS

(1) THE COTE-HARDIE [1320–1450], worn by women over the kirtle, and similar in cut to those of the men, being close-fitting, low-necked and long. Either buttoned down the front to below the waist (as with men's), or made with a low neck and put on over the head.

27. 14TH CENTURY, 1ST HALF

(a) Sleeveless surcoat over kirtle. Apron. Hood open in front; small liripipe. (b) Pouch at belt. (c) Cote-hardie. Veil and fillet. (d) Apron over kirtle. (e) Sleeved surcoat over kirtle. Closed veil.

a

b

c

28. 14TH CENTURY, 1ST HALF

(a) Kirtle. Barbette and fillet. (b) Sleeved surcoat. Veil and wimple
(c) Garde-corps.

Sleeves elbow-length, expanding into small or large tongue-shaped hanging flaps.

Fitchets, i.e. the vertical placket holes in the skirt, were fairly common.

No girdle worn.

(2) THE SLEEVED SURCOAT, loose and unshaped, continued in use. It was sometimes made with side vents.

Length: (*a*) To the ground, or

(*b*) Sometimes just below the knees.

Sleeves with wide expansion below elbows.

(3) THE SLEEVELESS SURCOAT continued in use, occasionally slit up at the sides for a short distance above the hem.

No girdle.

3. OUTER GARMENTS

(1) SHORT PELISSONS.

(2) CLOAKS. Long full and hooded, worn for warmth when travelling.

Mantles with costly linings, and loosely tied with tasselled cords springing from jewelled attachments, were ceremonial.

(3) THE GARDE-CORPS was occasionally worn by women as an outer wrap.

4. STOCKINGS

Unchanged. Gartered above or below the knees.

Materials, wool or linen, and coarse wool for the poor.

5. FOOTWEAR

Shoes in the style and decoration used by men.

6. HEADWEAR

(1) VEILS AND WIMPLES continued to be worn in the former style.

(2) VEILS ALONE, or secured by a fillet placed low on the head, began to be arranged thus: The veil was pulled into the shape of the head (coif-like) and securely pinned in place, leaving two

29. 14TH CENTURY, 1ST HALF

(a) Sleeveless surcoat. Flowing veil, and hair net. (*c.* 1340.) (b) (c)
Hoods with small liripipes (b) (1340). (c) Shows buttons for closing
hood. Worn over veil and wimple. (Early 14th c.) (d) Veil moulded
over hair bosses, flowing ends. Wimple. Sleeved surcoat. (*c.* 1340.)
(e) Barbette and fillet visible over top of head. (*c.* 1310.)

long ends to fall behind as streamers. When no fillet was worn the hair, enclosed in a net, might appear at the temples.

(3) THE BARBETTE AND FILLET continued in use during the early years of the century, usually worn with a crespine, and occasionally draped with a small veil.

The barbette was now frequently fixed over the head outside and not under the hair net.

The fillet was usually fairly shallow.

The crespine (or hair net) was often brightly coloured e.g. red with white spots.

(4) CRESPINE AND FILLET (without barbette). The crespine was brought well down over the hair, which was massed in coils round the ears; the fillet, worn low, crossed the upper part of the forehead. 'More than half a basinfull of pins' used to secure these headdresses.

(5) HOODS were now worn by all for travelling and warmth, and by country women at all times.

Liripipes were short or long.

Women's hoods were always open in front, and therefore not put on over the head like men's. For warmth the gorget might be folded across the neck or buttoned up from hem to chin. Hoods were often worn over another head-dress, such as veil and crespine.

7. HAIR

Plaited and coiled round the ears on each side, and usually covered by the crespine or completely hidden by the veil. This arrangement produced projections or, in contemporary language, 'bosses' on either side of the face.

Vertical plaits hugging the cheeks were fashionable from 1340 to 1400. A narrow fillet with rigid vertical strips to support the plaits, was common.

8. ACCESSORIES

Gloves worn by all classes.

Aprons worn domestically and by country-women. Usually large, without bib, and tied round the waist. A band of

30. 14TH CENTURY, 1ST HALF
HEADDRESSES

(a) Crespine, barbette and fillet. (b) Crespine alone. (c) Crespine and fillet. (d) Hairdressing—coiling a plait above the ear. Lady inspecting result in mirror. (1340.)

a

b

31. 14TH CENTURY, 1ST HALF

(a) Vertical plaits, with supporting side pieces from fillet. (Style 1340–1400.) (b) Vertical plaits partially covered by veil and wimple. (1349.)

embroidery along the upper border, below the waist belt, was very common.

Jewellery. Rings, brooches, buckles, etc. as for men.

Heraldic motifs, and even short mottoes, were embroidered on ceremonial cloaks, as with men's.

CONTEMPORARY DESCRIPTION of a tournament, tempus Edward III, is appended. 'These tournaments are attended by many ladies of the first rank and greatest beauty, but not always of the most untainted reputation. They are dressed in particoloured tunics, one half being of one colour and the other half of another, with short hoods and liripipes which are wrapped about their heads like cords; their girdles are handsomely ornamented with gold and silver and they wear short swords or daggers before them in pouches, a little below the navel; and thus habited they are mounted on the finest horses that can be procured and ornamented with the richest furniture' (Henry Knighton, 1348).

Second Half of
the Fourteenth Century

MEN

1. THE GIPON (called doublet for civilian use by 1370s).

Continued to be tight-fitting, waisted, and buttoned or laced down the front.

The changes were:

    (*a*) Extra padding in front, giving a 'pouter-pigeon' effect.

    (*b*) The skirt grew steadily shorter, scantily covering the hips; and was usually joined by a seam to the body. Short side vents that could be buttoned were sometimes present.

The sleeves, still tight and buttoned from elbow to wrist, or sewn up. (Chaucer speaks of 'with a threde bastynge my sleeves', using 'a sylver nedyl'.)

New Variations

    (*a*) Sleeves, usually extending to the knuckles, expanding into a funnel shape.

    (*b*) The 'grande assiette', a form of sleeve much rarer in England than (*a*). This was cut so that the sleeve was inserted with a circular seam overlapping the front and back of the bodice, plate-wise.

The Neck remained low and round until *c.* 1420. A standing collar followed.

Estaches, i.e., strings, were now sewn to the under surface of the gipon below for the attachment of the hose, formerly suspended from the girdle of the braies (drawers).

The gipon, especially during the last quarter of the fourteenth

a

b

32. 14TH CENTURY, 2ND HALF

(a) Gipon with ornamental buttons, sleeves buttoned from elbow to
knuckles, knightly girdle. Dagged mantle buttoned on right shoulder.
Long hose. Ankle shoes with inner lacing. (*c.* 1350). (b) Cote-hardie
with long tippets. Shoulder cape. (*c.* 1350).

century, was sometimes worn without an over-garment, in which case it was belted.

2. THE COTE-HARDIE

The changes were:

(*a*) The front fastening extended from neck to hem.

(*b*) The sleeves were fairly close fitting to the elbow; the hanging flap became longer and narrower, and was known as a '*Tippet*'. French 'Coudière'.

(*c*) The Tippet was a straight band of material, generally white, which hung down to the knees or lower. Usually a similar white band encircled the sleeve forming a cuff at the elbow.

(*d*) The length rapidly diminished like that of the gipon, and the cote-hardie skirt was often dagged.

(*e*) During the last quarter of the fourteenth century the cote-hardie, still closely buttoned down the front, developed a collar.

Just at the close of the century long sleeves, buttoned down the forearm and expanding into a funnel shape over the hands, came into fashion. The garment gradually became almost indistinguishable from the short Houppelande (which see for description), with similar varying sleeves and collar shapes. But the belt of the cote-hardie was worn round the hips; that of the houppelande was worn round the waist.

The buttoned front of the cote-hardie ceased about 1400, when pleats usually hid the fastenings, which were probably hooks and eyes.

From 1390 to 1410, the cote-hardie was worn extremely short, ending at the fork, a fashion favoured by the 'exquisite', though not by others.

The *girdle* was worn over the cote-hardie round the hips, and was often very ornate and long.

The knightly girdle [1350–1410], worn by nobles over the cote-hardie, was a broad belt of highly decorative metal plaques joined together and fastened in front by an ornamental buckle.

33. 14TH CENTURY, 2ND HALF

(a) Gipon horizontally quilted; (p. 100) sleeves of 'grande assiette' form
(p. 78 (b)). Plumed hat. (*c.* 1360). (b) Gipon horizontally quilted. (p. 100)
Hood and buttoned cape. (*c.* 1350). (c) Gipon very waisted and padded
over chest. Hood with dagged facial opening and long liripipe.
Parti-coloured soled hose, pointed feet. (Late 14th c.)

Always worn at hip level, and therefore probably sewn or hooked on.

3. THE GARNACHE

Its use continued, usually with the characteristic small tongue-shaped lapels at the neck.

4. THE HOUPPELANDE (1380 to 1450, after which known as the Gown). The name given to a new type of gown, a characteristic upper garment from 1380 and throughout the following century.

General description:

All made on the same principle, varying only in detail. Narrow above, steadily expanding downwards; thus fitting the shoulders but falling below into gradually deepening tubular folds which were kept in place at the waist by the belt. It was cut from four pieces, with a seam front and back and one on each side. These seams were often left open for a short distance from the hem, making *vents* in front, behind, and at the sides, the number varying according to fancy [1380–1440].

Length: (a) Long, to the ground (ceremonial).

(b) Short, knee length.

(c) Any intermediate length.

The Neck had a very high upright collar expanding like the neck of a carafe and reaching to the ears or higher behind, sometimes merging with the headgear.

Its edge, often closely dagged, gave a marked resemblance to a ruff. The collar was hooked or buttoned in front from chin to chest. Very occasionally it was fastened behind, or the top buttons in front were left undone and the collar partially turned down.

This gown was put on over the head.

Towards 1400 it was sometimes buttoned all down the front.

Sleeves. Funnel shaped, widening from the shoulders downwards and ending in an immense aperture, the lower edge sometimes reaching the ground. The upper edge never fell beyond the wrist, leaving the hand free. Sleeves frequently dagged.

82

Dagging (or Jagging) (used after 1170, widely fashionable from 1380 to 1440 but continued off and on to 1500).

This form of decoration, now extremely fashionable and complicated, consisted in cutting almost any border of any garment into elaborate scallops in the shape of leaves, tongues, fringes and compound vandykes, sometimes added as appliqué work in overlapping series. It was particularly applied to the houppelande, being used for the hem, up and down the slits of the skirt, round the huge sleeve opening, and very fully round the top of the collar, producing the ruff-like effect already mentioned.

Epaulettes, dagged and embroidered, were very common.

'May not a man see as in our days the sinful costly array of clothing, and namely in too much superfluity . . . that maketh it so dear, to the harm of the people, not only the cost of the embroidering, the disguising, indenting or barring, ounding (waving), paling, winding or bending, and suchlike waste of cloth in vanity; but there is also the costly furring in their gowns, so much pouncing of chisel to make holes, so much dagging of shears, with the superfluity in length of the aforesaid gowns, trailing in the dung and in the mire, on horse and eke on foot, as well of man as of woman.' (Chaucer, 'The Parson's Tale'.)

CEREMONIAL MANTLES continued.

5. OUTDOOR GARMENTS

(1) CLOAKS continued in use to the end of the century, after which they ceased to be fashionable, but were chiefly worn for travelling.

(2) SHOULDER CAPES [1330–1430], usually heavily dagged, continued in use.

(3) CAPES, thigh length, cut on the circle, with low collars and closely buttoned down the front, also occurred at this period.

6. LEGWEAR

HOSE reached the fork. Round the upper border were pairs of eyelet holes, through which strings (French 'estaches'), from the under side of the gipon, were threaded and tied in a single bow.

83

34. 14TH CENTURY, 2ND HALF

(a) Short houppelande; high dagged collar. 'Hood-turban' head-dress (p. 87 (2)). Parti-coloured soled hose. (Late 14th c.) (b) Dagged gipon. Parti-coloured hose and shoes. (c. 1374). (c) Gipon with side vents. Knightly girdle. (2nd half 14th c.) (d) Cote-hardie with dagged tippets. Dagged shoulder cape. Hood thrown back; long liripipe. (2nd half 14th c.) (e) Long houppelande with side vents. (c. 1395–96). (f) Short houppelande. Parti-coloured and piked soled hose. (c. 1395–96).

Hose were made of a stretchable material cut on the cross with a seam down the back.

Parti-coloured hose were common until 1420.

'... their hose are of two colours, or pied with more, which they tie to their paltocks (i.e. gipon) with white lachets called herlots.' (Anonymous author of Eulogium. A History from the Creation to 1413).

Joined Hose, appearing at the very end of the century, are described in the next section.

The shape of the 'feet' followed the anatomical outline, but the point opposite the big toe was slightly increased.

Long exaggerated pikes [1395–1410] (i.e. pointed toes) appeared at the end of the century, the toes being stuffed with tow, moss or hay.

Soled hose continued in use.

7. FOOTWEAR

(1) SHOES. Similar to those of the first half of the century.

(*a*) Fastened by lacing on inner or outer side with close fit round ankle.

(*b*) With buckled ankle strap and short or long uppers.

Towards 1360 they began to be sharply pointed, and punched out designs were popular. 'Paule's windows carven on his shoes' (Chaucer). Though not seen in contemporary illustrations, a fashion for long piked shoes was attempted but did not become established until about thirty years later. 'No knight under the estate of a lord, esquire or gentleman, nor any other person, shall wear any shoes or boots having pikes or points exceeding the length of two inches, under the forfeiture of forty pence; and every shoemaker who shall make pikes for shoes or boots beyond the length stated in this statute shall forfeit for every offence the sum of forty pence.' (Sumptuary law, Edward III).

In 1395 *Piked Shoes* or (Fr.) *'Poulaines'*, with long spear-like points, came into fashion. The higher the rank the longer the points, both for the gentry and their attendants [1395–1410, revived later].

35. 14TH CENTURY, 2ND HALF

(a) Shoes with long uppers and buckled ankle strap. (b) (c) Shoes with low uppers and buckled ankle strap. (d) to (h) Shoes with long uppers and ankle straps; long pointed toes, and punched out designs.

(2) BOOTS and Buskins, similar to those of the first half of the century, followed the piked fashion to a less degree.

Short Boots for walking, were laced or buttoned as in the first half. Hooked on the outer side (*c.* 1395) was a new method of fastening.

(3) GALOCHES or Clogs.

(4) PATTENS, wooden soles with leather straps, began to be worn with shoes to raise the foot from the ground in muddy weather (For description see p. 111). 'Their shoes and pattens are snouted and picked' ('Eulogium Historiarum' *c.* 1420).

8. HEADWEAR

(1) THE HOOD with liripipe, as formerly.

(2) THE 'HOOD-TURBAN', a descriptive name only, for a new way of wearing the hood which entirely changed its appearance (1380–1420. Very common 1390–1410). The *facial opening* was now fitted on to the head, the edges rolled back, and the liripipe, if long, twisted round the crown, an end dangling on one side.

The *gorget* fell in folds to the opposite side, or if of stiff material it stood erect, in whole or part, fanwise above the head. Its edge, generally dagged, gave it a marked resemblance to a cock's comb. There were many variations of this according to taste.

Materials as formerly.

(3) The COIF continued in use.

(4) HATS.

The various styles of hat worn in the first half of the century persisted, but tended to become more decorative by added trimming. Two new styles emerged in the last decade (1) The padded roll, usually dagged. (2) The bag-shaped crown. Both are described in the next period, when they were common.

(*a*) *Plumes* began to appear, mostly of dyed ostrich or peacock feathers. One or two were fixed upright in front or behind, being attached to the base of the crown by a brooch or jewelled ornament. 'In none of the old romances, replete as they are with descriptions of dress and armour, is there any allusion to feathers earlier than the middle of the fourteenth century,' (Planché's *Cyclopaedia*).

36. 14TH CENTURY, 2ND HALF
HEADWEAR

(a) (b) (c) Diagrammatic representations of conversion of hood.
(a) Hood; (b) hood with facial opening for head, and (c) final result,
producing—(d) (f) 'Hood-turbans' with liripipe twisted round head.
(e) High crowned plumed hat. (g) Bag-crowned hat worn over dagged
hood. (h) 'Hood-turban', and early houppelande.

(*b*) *Hat bands* with decorative designs became popular.

Materials for hats. Felt, beaver, or any showy textile.

Hats were sometimes slung behind by attached strings. 'His hat heng at his back down by a las' (Chaucer).

9. HAIR

Either

(*a*) From a centre parting the hair hung down to the upper or lower part of the neck.

or

(*b*) Hair cut fairly short all over, without a parting.

Face clean shaven, or beard and moustache, usually without side whiskers.

10. ACCESSORIES

Knightly Girdles.

Daggers.

Pouches.

Jewellery, such as gold head-circlets.

Gloves, for all classes.

Handkerchiefs. The word handkerchief is not met with until the sixteenth century. Previous to that period it was called '*hand cloth*' or *hand-coverchief,* or mokador. Their origin attributed to Richard II, e.g. 'little pieces of material made for giving to the lord King for carrying in his hand to wipe and cleanse his nose' (John Hervey's *The Plantagenets*).

Note on Mourning

About the middle of the fourteenth century black became more generally recognised as the symbol of grief.

Previously one black garment would be worn over ordinary coloured clothing.

Second Half of
the Fourteenth Century

WOMEN

1. THE KIRTLE or GOWN

Continued with close-fitting bodice and full skirt, and girdle worn low.

> *He seeth her shape forthwith all*
> *Her body round, her middle small.*
>
> JOHN GOWER

Sleeves were tight-fitting to the wrist, and there expanded like mittens over the hand as far as the knuckles.

Buttoned from above or below elbow to hand (1330 to end of Middle Ages).

2. OVER GARMENTS

(1) THE COTE-HARDIE continued as in the first half of the century, but the short flaps hanging from the tight elbow sleeves changed to long streamers or *Tippets*. These were similar to the men's except that, like the garment itself, the tippets were always very long, often trailing on the ground. No girdle was worn unless the cote-hardie replaced the kirtle immediately beneath the sideless surcoat.

(2) THE SIDELESS SURCOAT (1360 to 1500; ceremonially up to 1520) was an important and characteristic garment from now to the end of the Middle Ages. It developed from the sleeveless surcoat. Its distinguishing feature was the large side openings stretching from shoulders to hips. They extended low enough to reveal the underlying *knightly girdle* or ordinary belt, whichever

37. 14TH CENTURY, 2ND HALF

(a) Sleeved surcoat with fitchets. Kirtle sleeves emerging. (*c.* 1370.)
(b) Cote-hardie with fitchets; long tippets to sleeve (*c.* 1364). (c) Sideless surcoat with plackard; side opening shows girdle of kirtle. (1378–80.)
(d) Sideless surcoat, and 'cushion' head-dress. (*c* 1380.)

was worn. The gap was often wide enough to leave only a narrow strip of material down the front.

A *Plackard* was the name given to the front portion forming a stomacher curved in to the waist, and usually rounded below giving a variation in form. It was sometimes made of fur.

From the hips this surcoat hung in loose folds to the ground.

The *neck* was low and wide, the garment being slung from mere shoulder straps. To prevent its falling off there is some evidence that it was fastened at the waist behind the plackard to the gown beneath. Its *decoration* comprised a row of buttons or jewels down the midline in front. *Fur borders* and lining were usual. 'In the summer it were better away entirely because it only serveth for a hiding place for the fleas' (Knight of the Tour Landry. Advice to his Daughters) (1371-72).

(3) A LOOSE SLEEVELESS SURCOAT, sometimes having side vents, was still worn as a domestic style or by the poorer classes.

(4) A LOOSE, SLEEVED SURCOAT, slit up at each side from hem to waist, without a girdle, was also a domestic style still in use.

(5) MANTLES, chiefly ceremonial, long and much decorated, were loosely fastened across the chest by jewelled bands or tasselled cords. These mantles were sometimes parti-coloured and embroidered all over with various devices.

3. OUTER GARMENTS

(1) HOODED CLOAKS, for travelling or riding (Ladies rode side-saddle; countrywomen astride).

(2) SHORT PELISSONS continued in use.

4. STOCKINGS

Reaching above the knee, and gartered above or below.

> *Here hosen weren of fine skarlet redde*
> *Ful straite y-teyed.*
> Chaucer's Wife of Bath.

5. FOOTWEAR

SHOES as for the men, but never with long pikes.

a

b

38. 14TH CENTURY, 2ND HALF

(a) Kirtle with front lacing. Low girdle. Long mantle. Goffered veil;
the so-called 'nebula' head-dress. (c. 1370.) (b) Sideless surcoat showing
plackard and kirtle belt on her left. Side plaits supported on extensions
from coronet. (c. 1388.)

a

b

c

39. 14TH CENTURY, 2ND HALF
HEADWEAR

(a) Goffered veil, ruched only round forehead. (c. 1393.) (b) Goffered veil worn over fillet. (c. 1391.) (c) Goffered veil, the ruching forming an arch round the face. (c. 1370.)

6. HEAD WEAR

Veils and *Wimples* continued, but more ornamental veils began now to appear.

(1) The GOFFERED VEIL or NEBULA HEADDRESS [1350–1420], descriptive names assigned later. Made of a half-circle of linen, draped over the head. Possibly several layers were used at times. The straight edge, decorated by a *broad goffered frill* resembling a ruff, formed an arch round the face, ending at the temples or descending to the chin or below. Thence it was continued un-goffered, to meet the circular border which draped the shoulders. The latter might be goffered also in whole or in part.

The goffered 'arch' was sometimes square, covered with orna-mental network, and worn over a fillet which was visible in front only across the forehead.

(2) An ORNAMENTAL FILLET, with attached side-pieces re-sembling carved or openwork pillars hugging the cheeks in front of the ears, gave the face a very square shape. These side 'pillars' were hollow, a tress of hair being drawn through each. The rest of the hair was covered by a crespine or veil which hung down at the back.

Coronets, when worn, were usually shaped to fit over the side pieces.

(3) An ORNAMENTAL FILLET, or CORONET WITHOUT SIDE PIECES. Worn with crespine or veil as in (2), or very occasionally without either. But a vertical plait of hair was fixed in position on each side of the face, in place of the 'side pillars'.

Head-dresses (2) and (3) gradually merged, at the end of the century, into the more elaborate structures of the next century, built upon the same principle.

(4) 'CUSHION HEAD-DRESS' [1380–1415], a descriptive name only for a *padded roll* worn over a hair net; a fashion appearing near the close of this century and typical of the next.

(5) HOODS and HATS continued in use for homely wear or for travelling.

(6) CRESPINES or HAIR NETS, also known as CAULS, were very usual with all types of head covering. 'A fret of golde she hadde next her heer' Chaucer, Legend of Good Women.

40. 14TH CENTURY, 2ND HALF

(a) Side and top view of headdress, showing ornamental network covering goffered veil. Fillet worn outside veil. (b) Front and side views of fillet with side pillars enclosing the hair. Veil shows behind neck. (p. 95 (2)).

7. HAIR

As formerly, coiled, braided or crimped round the ears, partly concealed under crespine or head-dress, if not hidden under the veil.

Fashionable ladies, from 1340 to 1400, often arranged their hair in vertical plaits which were passed straight down in front of the ears from the fillet to the angle of the jaw, and sometimes held in place by a net. The ends were turned up and hidden under the head-dress.

Shaved front hair, to produce a broad high forehead, was a new mode [1370–1480].

The hair was frequently dyed saffron colour.

Eyebrow plucking and face painting became fashionable [1370–1480]. '. . . fair daughters, see that you pluck not away the hairs from your eyebrows nor from your temples nor from your foreheads, to make them appear higher than Nature ordained'. (Advice to his daughters by the Knight of la Tour Landry, 1371–72).

8. ACCESSORIES

As for the first half of the century.

Jewellery very abundant. 'I saw a woman . . . her head was adorned with so rich a crown that even the King had not a better. On al her fyv fyngers ful richely she rynged' (Vision of Piers Plowman).

Knightly girdles.

Decorative effects were becoming more marked; all primary colours were in use, especially green.

Dagging was less frequent on women's garments.

The *fashionable Posture* for women was to thrust forward the abdomen with the back curved, producing a 'slouching' attitude.

First Half of the Fifteenth Century

MEN

1. THE DOUBLET.

(This term used from 1400 to 1670), 'I be-quethe to Richard my servant . . . and a doblet' (will of John Solas 1418)—corresponding to the gipon. Worn over the shirt as a tight-fitting, well waisted garment; clinging to the hips it barely reached to the thighs. It was padded throughout with extra thickness over the chest. Made up in eight pieces, with a centre seam down the back and a seam round the waist. It was rarely worn uncovered after 1412.

Belted at hip level when worn alone.

Fastenings: (a) By lacing down the front [1400–1450].

(b) By buttons or hooks and eyes [after 1425].

The Neck

(a) Continued round and collarless for 15 to 20 years [to 1420]

(b) Then collars were added [1420–1490], being close-fitting, and (from 1450 to 1490) stand-up, with a V opening in front, cut with points under the chin, sometimes laced across.

Sleeves

(a) Close-fitting to the wrist, extending to the knuckles, and buttoned up to the elbow, the buttonholes being placed as near the edge as possible and the buttons having long shanks [1360–1420].*

(b) 'À grandes assiettes' (see fourteenth century, second half) [1360–1440].

The doublet was now supplied with pairs of *eyelet holes* round

* Ending at the wrist from 1420 on.

98

a

b

c

41. 15TH CENTURY, 1ST HALF

(a) Long houppelande, buttoned down chest; tubular sleeves; doublet
sleeves emerging. Shoulder belt for dagger. Hood thrown back. Instep
strap shoes. (*c.* 1400–5.) (b) Long houppelande, buttoned throughout.
Belt knotted and buckled. Buttons to mantle, and hood thrown back.
(*c.* 1400.) (c) Houppelande, lined and edged with fur; standing collar
with V opening. Front vent to skirt. Bagpipe sleeves. High shoes with
inner lacing. Bowl crop hair. (*c.* 1437.)

the hem corresponding to similar pairs round the upper border of the hose; the latter were attached to the doublet by ties called *points* threaded through these openings (See section on Hose).

Materials. For ordinary use: broadcloth, linen, fustian, sometimes leather.

For special occasions; damask, satin or velvet. Mixed materials were employed when the doublet was mostly hidden by the gown (e.g. body of plain material with collar and sleeves of a more ornate stuff) (Commonest from 1430 to 1460).

Quilting

The lines of stitching were:

(*a*) Vertical (usually military).

(*b*) Horizontal (usually civil).

(*c*) Invisible (also civil), having a flat surface, the quilting confined to the lining.

2. THE COTE-HARDIE (Sometimes called a Jacket).

Still close-fitting and very waisted, but now often made with gathers in front and behind.

Fastened invisibly, probably hooked behind under the pleats.

Length. Very short, at first barely reaching the fork (among the ultra-fashionable, 1390 to 1410). Knee length [1410–1450].

Neck. At first a high stand-up collar [1380–1420].

No collar after 1420, when this was transferred to the doublet.

Sleeves

(*a*) Close-fitting with bugle cuffs reaching the knuckles; buttoned to elbows.

(*b*) Other sleeves resembling those described under 'Houppe-lande' (q.s.) into which the short cote-hardie merged.

Belt worn at hip level.

3. THE HOUPPELANDE, or Gown.

Though essentially the same in structure, it now showed many changes in detail. Vents continues until about 1440.

The *closed gown* implied that it had no vents [1440–1550]; it was closer fitting and not put on over the head, being fastened

42. 15TH CENTURY, 1ST HALF

(a) (b) Short houppelandes, with closed hanging sleeves. (1409 and 1416.) (c) Ditto. Third man wearing one sleeve normally. Short boots with outer lacing and pattens. (c. 1440.) (d) Long houppelande with high dagged collar and epaulettes. Wide funnel sleeves showing fur lining. Large necklace. Dagged head roll (p. 115 (3)). (c. 1410.) (e) Houppelande with hanging sleeves having no opening at wrist. Hood with liripipe twisted round head. (c. 1433.) (f) Houppelande with high dagged collar and wide funnel sleeves. (c. 1410.)

down the front from neck to hem by buttons or more often by hooks and eyes, mostly concealed under folds which were stitched down into place under the belt.

Fitchets were very occasionally present.

Arrangement of folds

(a) Eight folds were the commonest (two in front, two behind, and two at each side) [1410–1440].

(b) Like massed organ pipes, front and back, for the whole length, with plain smooth sides [1440 on].

The Neck

(1) With Collar [1380–1425].

(a) Very tall 'bottle neck' collar, usually dagged, buttoned up to the chin from chest. Sometimes this style was closely buttoned from chin to hem, contrary to the usual custom [1380–1410].

(b) The same shape, but lower, and having a V opening at the throat [1400–1425].

(c) A large turned-down collar spreading flat over the shoulders [1410–1425].

(d) A very low upright collar with rounded edges sloping to a wide V in front, resembling the doublet collar which showed above it [1425–1460].

This fashion overlapped that of no collar.

(2) Without Collar (1425 to 1500. Rare earlier in England.).

The neckline varied, but was generally edged with fur regardless of the season.

(a) Fitting in front and sloping to a V behind [1420–1480].

(b) Fitting in front and sloping to a U behind [1450–1470].

(c) Fitting behind and sloping to a V in front [1430–1465].

(d) Sloping to a V in front and behind (off and on).

(e) Plain round neck [1425–1500].

Sleeves

Three types: open, closed or hanging (open or closed).

(1) Open Sleeve

(a) An immense funnel-shape, as previously described (1380 to 1420. Ceremonially up to 1450).

(b) A plain cylindrical sleeve of equal width from shoulder

43. 15TH CENTURY (1st half)

(a) Houppelandes showing V necks, side vent, and belts at different levels. (c. 1425-40.) (b) Long houppelande with wide funnel-shaped sleeves. Collar open in front. Hat with bag-shaped crown. (c. 1408.) (c) Short houppelande with 'closed' hanging sleeves. Neck ornament. Doublet collar appearing above. (c. 1429.) (d) Very short houppelande, bag-pipe sleeves and high dagged collar. (c. 1408.) (e) Very long cere-monial houppelande, wide funnel-shaped sleeves. Round neck with doublet collar rising above it. (c. 1415-20.)

to wrist; largely worn by peasants, but became fashionable
c. 1430 [1400–1500].

(c) A short sleeve which was in effect the cylindrical sleeve
rolled up to the elbow level, giving a cuff-like appearance,
especially as the lining was usually of a different colour
(1400 off and on to 1480s).

(2) The Closed Sleeve (1405 to 1500. Occasionally seen up to
1520.) This was very full, and cut in one piece with a seam down
the front, and buttoned at the wrist. It might be gathered or
plain at the shoulder, and gathered into a wristband below; or
shaped to the wrist without a cuff. Or any combination of the
two.

Variations:

(a) *The Bagpipe Sleeve,* also called the *Pokys* (1400 to 1430s.
Very popular c. 1410). Enormously wide, and shaped to form
a hanging bag or pouch, and often used as such. 'May rightly
be called the Devil's receptacles for whatever could be stolen
was popped into them' (Gough, Vol. 1 p. clxiii).

(b) Much less full, but gathered to form a 'kick-up' at the
shoulder, and gathered below into a wristband [after 1445].

(3) Hanging Sleeves

All had an opening in the form of a slit down the front of the
upper part, allowing the arm (in its doublet sleeve) to be passed
through at will.

(a) The closed variety, full and gathered or shaped into a
cuff [1400–1520s], being much commoner during the first half
of the fifteenth century. A rare type had no opening at the
wrist, and resembled a hanging balloon, a German mode
which spread to France and England [1430–1435].

(b) The open variety, the sleeve being long and cylindrical.

Decoration of Houppelande

(a) Fur borders to neck, hem, vents and wrists were characteristic of this period, and were used all the year round
[1420–1515]. After 1515 these borders were largely relegated
to ecclesiastical vestments.

Fur linings common in winter.

The furs used, in order of popularity, among the wealthy:

44. 15TH CENTURY, 1ST HALF

(a) Huke, belted round both panels. (b) Huke, belted round front panel, the back hanging loose. (c) Huke, unbelted and dagged.

sable, ermine, civet, beaver, grise, fox and lamb. Ermine studded with black tails was reserved for royalty.

The poorer classes used hare, coney, cat and red squirrel.

(*b*) Dagging

(*c*) Embroidery

(*d*) Woven patterns in damask or figured velvet. The designs were:

(i) Dotted patterns of circles, stars, wheels, roses or asters [common 1400–1450].

(ii) Trailing designs, usually very massive. All colours were used [very common *c*. 1430].

Materials for Houppelandes

Wool, velvet, satin, damask.

Linings

In summer. Satin, silk, taffeta, linen or plain cloth.

In winter. Fur or cloth.

Houppelandes were rarely unlined.

Quotation from Thomas Occleve '. . . an evil to see one walking in gownes of scarlet twelve yards wide, with sleeves reaching to the ground, and lined with fur worth twenty pounds or more. . . . The taylors must soon shape their garments in the open field for want of room to cut them in their own houses; because that man is best respected who bears upon his back, at one time, the greatest quantity of cloth and of fur.'

4. THE BELT

This was essential all through the first half of the fifteenth century. A symbol of degradation was to deprive a man of his belt. Very rarely, and as a sign of humility, a beltless gown was worn.

Position

(*a*) At waist level [1400–1500].

(*b*) Sometimes below [1400–1460].

Materials. Leather or spun silk coloured (black, white, green, blue, vermilion and other shades).

Buckles for fastening belt. Often richly worked, of gold, silver, iron or copper. In shape oval, oblong or square; single commoner than double. Usually worn centrally in front, but could be placed on either side of midline.

Some belts were tied in a knot after being buckled, and some had a long hanging end reaching to mid-calf [1400–1425. Very common *c.* 1425].

Objects slung from the belt

(*a*) Purse or pouch of leather of varying designs.

(*b*) A knife or dagger; often fixed to the back or the front of the purse; when no pouch was worn the dagger was hung by a sling or small chain fastened to the belt at any position.

CEREMONIAL MANTLES continued.

5. OUTER GARMENTS

(1) THE CLOAK. Rare after 1400.

(2) THE SHOULDER CAPE, usually dagged, worn independently of the hood [1330–1430. Off and on later].

(3) THE HUKE [1400–1450. Rare later]. Originally worn over armour, became a civilian garment, replacing the cloak for outdoor wear. Worn over the gown in winter and over the doublet in summer, was of tabard design, and put on over the head. Generally belted, and occasionally sleeved.

Two types:

(*a*) The *riding huke,* short, reaching to mid-thigh; slit up in front for convenience in the saddle.

(*b*) The *pedestrian huke;* knee-length or a little longer; no front slit.

N.B. The huke of ground length came in during the second half of the fifteenth century.

6. LEGWEAR

Two types of hose: (1) Separate like stockings. (2) Joined, combining stockings and breeches in one garment, like modern 'tights'.

(1) SEPARATE HOSE.

Though far less common these were never entirely discarded;

45. 15TH CENTURY, 1ST HALF

(a) Tongued separate hose with points which have given way. (b) (c) Ditto. Shows eyelet holes in doublet, and points trussed and untrussed (d) Labourer's separate hose, turned down and footless. (e) Doublet, laced down front. Joined hose with codpiece, and neatly trussed.

worn especially by labourers and inferiors. Made very long, with a top edge round or tongued for easier attachment to the front of the doublet. The upper border was pierced with eyelet holes through which strings were threaded and then passed through similar holes in the doublet. These, acting as suspenders, were called 'points'. The procedure was known as 'trussing the points'. (See section on Joined Hose.)

Points being very apt to break, labourers used few, especially at the back, or none at all, and instead rolled down their hose below the knee. In summer peasants working in the fields discarded their hose, wearing shirts and braies only.

Short hose, gartered below the knee and occasionally footless were also worn by labourers.

(2) JOINED HOSE (1400 to 1515, after which the design changed).

These became inevitable with the wearing of shorter garments. The long legs, reaching to the fork, were united, and continued upwards over the hips forming 'tights', which at first barely covered the seat; reaching the waist by the end of the century.

They were fastened to the doublet, now very short, by *trussing* the points; the lower border of the doublet was pierced by eyelet holes in pairs corresponding to similar pairs round the top of the hose. The strings ('*points*') were tipped with ornamental metal tabs ('*aiglets*'), which were threaded through these holes and tied in a single loop.

Points were usually of leather. 'The inventory of a London haberdasher, 1378, listed a gross of "poynts of red leather", the earliest noted reference.' (Linthicum) (Double bows were never made).

Arrangement of eyelet holes in doublet and hose: All through the century the numbers varied from two to twelve pairs, the commonest being nine (Two pairs in front, three at each side, one pair behind).

The *Codpiece* [1408-1575], was a small pouch formed by a front flap at the fork, fastened by ties (Cod, an old term for bag).

Both separate and joined hose might be:

(*a*) Footed

(b) Stirrups only

(c) Without either (rare)

(d) Soled (worn without shoes), pattens being added in wet weather

The other forms were worn with shoes or boots.

Shape of the feet

(a) Piked, having long points, the ends stuffed with tow, moss or hay [1395–1410].

(b) As the shape of the foot, or rounded toes, later becoming pointed again [1410–1460].

(c) Return of long points ('piked') [1460–1480].

Materials

Hose were usually lined in part, and made of woollen material often reinforced with leather. 'Pair of hose of black kersey.' 'Pair of hose bound with leather.' 'Black hose vamped with leather.'

Colours

Often very bright. Parti-coloured hose were less popular in England than in France, and uncommon here from 1420 to 1470.

7. FOOTWEAR

All without raised heels.

(1) BOOTS OR BUSKINS

(a) *Short buskins* [1400–1500], reaching to calf, close-fitting (rarely, loose and baggy), fastened by lacing, buckles, or hooks and eyes, slightly to the outer side of the front midline. Made in one piece, with a seam down the back.

(b) *Long Buskins* [1400–1500. Commonest after 1450]. Reaching high up the thigh; only used on horseback until 1450.

Close-fitting, laced up on outer or inner side; a notch often made at the knee to facilitate bending the joint. Made in two pieces, the foot being joined to the leg.

Shape of foot, as for hose, i.e.

(i) Piked [1395–1410].

(ii) Natural shape, rounded or pointed toe [1410–1460].

(iii) Piked again [1460–1480].

Materials. Goat, sheep or cow-hide.

46. 15TH CENTURY, 1ST HALF

(a) Country shoes, one showing re-inforced heel and sole. (c. 1449.)
(b) Long riding buskin. (c) Buckled shoes. (c. 1418.) (d) Pattens, side,
upper and lower views. (e) Pattens (1434). (f) Piked shoes with inner
lacing. (c. 1405.)

Special Stockings were made for wearing inside the buskins and over the hose.

Leggings (or gaiters) bound by ties below the knee and round the ankle were worn by country folk.

(2) SHOES

All through the fifteenth century shoes were made like low boots, covering the foot and clasping the ankle, although open shoes fastened by ankle straps, of the fourteenth century style, continued in use for a few years.

Fastenings. Closed on inner or outer side, or down the centre by hooks, buttons, buckles, or lacing through eyelet holes (these *not* reinforced by metal). Frequently not fastened throughout, the portion round the ankle left gaping. Others were closed round the ankle, leaving a slit below to facilitate putting on the shoe.

Shoes were not indispensable, as soled hose, though usually worn indoors, were also worn out of doors.

Peasant's shoes were often reinforced with extra thickness at sole and heel.

Shape. As for boots.

(3) PATTENS [1400–1500. Known in 1390, but rare].

Worn with shoes, soled hose, and more rarely with buskins, to raise the wearer out of the mud.

Constructed with wooden soles, often raised at heel and toe, usually made of aspe[1] and painted white, shaped to the prevailing fashion of shoe but longer. Black leather straps were nailed on at each side (with four nails), and provided with buckles to fasten over the instep, or a 'saddle' over the instep secured them in position. Pattens were extremely fashionable from 1440 to 1460, and worn on all occasions indoors as well as out.

Leather pattens were occasionally worn by the nobility.

8. HEADWEAR

(1) THE HOOD [1160–1450, after which rare].

With closed gorget and long liripipe, and worn as a hood, continued for about 50 years. Small hoods, buttoned in front, and

[1] Aspe was used on account of its lightness. 'The most easy for wearing . . . of any timber that groweth'. (Linthicum).

47. 15TH CENTURY, 1ST HALF
HEADWEAR

(a) Hat, cone-shaped crown, brim turned up with an extra flourish in front. (p. 117 (i)). (Early 15th c.) (b) Hat with deep crown and divided brim turned up. (p. 115 (h)). (c. 1416.) (c) (f) Hats with high crowns and rolled brims. (p. 115 (a)). (Early 15th c.) (d) Chaperon with very long liripipe. Short houppelande with V opening in front (wide dagged sleeve unusual). (c. 1433.) (e) Peasant in small hat (p. 115 (c)). (c. 1416.) (g) Chaperon with bias twist to roundlet. No liripipe. (Early 15th c.)

usually worn thrown back forming a muffler round the neck, were now very fashionable. '. . . their hoods are little, tied under the chin and buttoned like the woman's, but set with gold, silver and precious stones' ('Eulogium Historiarum' *c.* 1420).

The *liripipe* on *hats* survived a little longer [till *c.* 1480]. It was occasionally used as a purse, the money being knotted in the closed end. The *liripipe* was sometimes *dagged* at this period [very common *c.* 1415].

The *hood-turban* continued in use (1390 to 1410, and unfashionably till 1420).

Materials and colours. Velvet, damask and russet. Black, green, purple, scarlet, blue and russet. 'Hood of russet velvet, with a tippet half of the same and half of blue velvet, lined with blue damask.'

'Hood of scarlet with a roll of purple velvet bordered with the same velvet.'

'Hood of russet velvet, the tippet lined with russet silk.'

'Hood of purple velvet without roll and tippet.'

'Hood of damask russet with tippet fastened with a lace of silk' (Sir John Fastolf's Wardrobe).

(2) THE CHAPERON (1420 to 1470, after which used by professions and older men).

A characteristic feature. Developed from the hood-turban, which was inconvenient to adjust. The new form was a ready-made headgear, consisting of three parts stitched into place:

(*a*) The *roundlet,* corresponding to the rolled facial brim, was a wheel-shaped pad stuffed with silk or cotton; either smooth and plain, or given a bias twist [common *c.* 1420] and, in this case, usually made with gorget but without liripipe.

(*b*) The *gorget,* was now transferred from the neck to the crown of the head, where it was sewn inside the roundlet and was long enough to form a capacious covering of two types:

(i) Sufficiently stiff to stand up, like a cock's comb sloping down from one side to the other (not from in front backwards). The 'tail' of the cock's comb overhung one side of the roundlet, with the liripipe overhanging the other.

(ii) Limp, so that the bulk of the material hung down in

48. 15TH CENTURY, 1ST HALF

(a) Large hat with hour-glass crown. (p. 115 (g)). (1434.) (b) Hair with bowl crop (style of 1410–1460). (c) Large ballooned crown. (p. 115 (f)). (c. 1435). (d) Hat with deep crown, and fur-covered divided brim turned up in front, down behind. (p. 115 (h)). (c. 1430.)

folds over the side opposite to the liripipe, which served as a counter-weight to the gorget.

When no liripipe was present the folds hung down like a curtain round the back of the head, from ear to ear.

(c) *The Liripipe.* Chaperons (and, later, hats with attached liripipes) were frequently worn suspended over one shoulder (preferably the left) with the liripipe in front and the hat behind. Both chaperons and hood-turbans could be worn over a plain hood.

(3) A PADDED ROLL [1395–1410], resembling a roundlet (but introduced earlier) and worn alone, was profusely dagged. It had the appearance of a wreath of closely packed leaves. Very popular, and generally worn with a jewelled ornament in front.

(4) The COIF continued in use, but became gradually limited to the professional classes as part of a habit.

A *deep skull cap* made of various materials, not tied under the chin and usually exposing the ears, followed the coif for wearing under any other headgear [c. 1425 on].

(5) HATS
A vary large variety, many having very distinctive dates.

(a) A tall form of 'top hat', broadening from below up, and often but not invariably flattened from front to back, or from side to side. The brim closely turned up or rolled [1394–1415].

(b) A bag-shaped crown flopping forward or sideways over a rolled brim [1394–1430s].

(c) A low, tapering crown, with small peaked brim turned up behind (thirteenth century to 1425).

(d) A round crown with large turned-up brim [1410–1470].

(e) A round crown with brim turned down or rolled [1400–1500].

(f) A large ballooned crown with moderately wide brim turned slightly up or down. Very popular in England [1430–1460].

(g) A large hour-glass crown, sometimes with projecting knob or spike on top, the brim flat or turned up [1430–1440].

(h) A deep round or flat-topped crown with brim divided into front and back portions, both sharply turned up and

49. 15TH CENTURY, 1ST HALF

(a) Hair with bowl crop, wispy forked beard. (b) Small hat with peaked front, and turned up behind. (c) Peasants' straw hats. (d) Hat with round crown, turned down; strings for travelling. (e) Top view of a bowl crop (*c.* 1446).

116

usually furred. Occasionally the back brim was turned down [1400–1440].

(*i*) Tall cone-shaped crown with brim rolled or projecting and slightly turned up behind and down in front or vice versa [1445–1485].

Strings were used to tie hats under the chin when travelling, or to allow them to be pushed off the head and slung on the shoulder.

Materials

Felt made from lamb, hare, rabbit or beaver; this last was the commonest, and was either rough or smooth. Beaver hats were usually lined with satin, cendal, velvet or scarlet cloth.

Straw hats were of various simple shapes.

Colours. Black, brown, grey, white or vermilion.

Trimmings

(*a*) Fur, very usual, the fur applied as a decoration to a felt body, often completely hiding the foundation.

The furs used were marten, miniver and astrachan.

(*b*) Plumes, hatbands, jewels, brooches and buckles.

9. HAIR

Early in the century to 1410 the hair was puffed out at the nape of the neck and on each side of the face, aided perhaps by pads.

The *Bowl Crop* (1410 to 1460, after which rather old-fashioned. Seen on tombs up to 1480), was extremely characteristic, becoming adopted almost universally. The hair was cut to resemble a shallow skull cap or inverted bowl with the rim only reaching to the upper level of the ears. Below this sharp line the head and neck were clean-shaven. The hair was brushed from a central spot on the crown to form a circular fringe round the head.

N.B. When long hair is shown in contemporary pictures it usually denotes imaginary characters; it was not a fashion in real life.

Short cropped hair was an unfashionable style appearing throughout the period.

Pointed or forked beards, the rest of the face being clean-shaven, or a mere wisp of a beard, were worn early in the century, but

a

b

50. 15TH CENTURY, 1ST HALF
(a) SS collar as worn and enlarged. (b) Pouch and dagger.

rarely with the bowl crop [1400–1415]. Later a *clean-shaven face* was the general rule, exceptions being rare [1415–1525].

10. ACCESSORIES

The Knightly Girdle [1360–1410] was worn at hip level over gipon or cote-hardie until 1410.

Jewelled Collars, often with personal devices, e.g. the 'SS collar' of the Lancastrians (1400 to 1550, but altered in design under the Tudors).

Folly Bells, an ornament composed of small bells hung

   (a) By chains from the girdle.

   (b) From a shoulder belt.

   (c) From a neck band.

Dagger and Pouch, as formerly.

Gloves, common to all.

Scarves sometimes worn.

Walking Sticks sometimes carried.

First Half of
the Fifteenth Century

WOMEN

1. THE KIRTLE

(Sometimes called by contemporaries a 'tunic', as in the trousseau of Princess Philippa, daughter of Henry IV.)

Worn next to the smock; was close-fitting, low-necked, with long tight sleeves usually reaching the knuckles like mittens, buttoned down forearm. The kirtle was buttoned or laced in front from neck to below waist or laced behind.

2. THE COTE-HARDIE

Continued as formerly till 1450, but was frequently hidden or replaced by the *Houppelande,* which became adopted by women in this country *c.* 1400.

3. THE SIDELESS SURCOAT (1360 to 1500, and to 1520 as state apparel and 1525 on effigies).

Continued unchanged to the end of the century, becoming then much less fashionable.

4. THE HOUPPELANDE or Gown [1400–1450s].

The Houppelande assumed the functions of a gown, during the fifteenth century.

This gown resembled the male houppelande in essentials; the minor differences being:

(1) The *belt* was worn at a high-waisted level.

(2) The gown was *always long;* on ceremonial occasions it

a   b   c

51. 15TH CENTURY, 1ST HALF

(a) Houppelande; high collar. Buttoned bagpipe sleeves. Kirtle sleeves emerging. Draped veil. (*c.* 1400.) (b) Mantle over kirtle, with buttoned sleeves extending to knuckles. Fillet. Templers above ears. Veil. (*c.* 1400.) (c) Houppelande with V neck (1440–60) and tubular sleeves. Veil draped over templers extending upwards and downwards.

swept the ground, with a train of varying length. The hem might measure as much as twelve yards round.

(3) *The Neck*

(*a*) A tall decanter-necked collar, generally without dagging. The garment was usually put on over the head and buttoned up from chest to chin, though often left open at the neck, leaving a high V opening; or the top buttons were left undone and the collar turned down to decrease the height. Rarely the buttons extended down the centre from chin to hem [1400–1410, rarely to 1420].

(*b*) A broad flat turned-down collar, sometimes of fur, and a short V opening in front; or fastened by lacing from neck to chest [1408–1440].

(*c*) A wide V opening front and back, extending down to the belt; edged with broad revers narrowing towards the point of the V, leaving the neck bare, or revealing part of the kirtle or cote-hardie [1440–1460].

(4) *Sleeves*

Similar to those of the male garment, but selective, e.g.

(*a*) Immense funnel-shaped; surviving a much longer period with women than with men [1400–1460].

(*b*) Plain tubular, of more or less equal width from shoulder to wrist [1400–1470].

(*c*) Bagpipe sleeve [1400–1430].

(*d*) Hanging sleeve of the open variety, being long and tubular. The closed variety was extremely rare, and the balloon shape unknown [1430–1500].

Loose Houppelandes, without belts and with closed necks, were sometimes worn by the elderly.

Ceremonial Mantles, long and full, cut on the circle; loosely fastened across the chest by tasselled cords or jewelled bands. Fur trimming along the borders was very common, and also fur linings.

'A mantle of blue cloth furred with pured miniver' (Trousseau of Princess Philippa, daughter of Henry IV 1406. *Archaeologia,* Vol. 67).

52. 15TH CENTURY (1st half)

(a) Elaborate fillet. Small templers. Bottle-neck collar of houppelande open at throat. (*c.* 1410.) (b) Trained cote-hardie with long tippets. Kirtle sleeves emerging. Circular padded roll headdress over hair net. (*c.* 1410.) (c) Houppelande with flat collar and bag-pipe sleeves. Laced as far as girdle. Veil draped over templers. (*c.* 1430.) (d) Trained houppelande with flat collar and trailing funnel-shaped sleeves. Wide padded roll with short veil. (Early 15th century.) (e) Cote-hardie with short tippets. Wired up veil. (Early 15th century.)

53. 15TH CENTURY, 1ST HALF

Fur-lined ceremonial mantle with heraldic motif, fastened by long
tasselled cord. Sideless surcoat trimmed with fur. Coronet shaped to fit
over rising templers, draped with small veil. Elaborate necklace. (1446).

54. 15TH CENTURY, 1ST HALF

(a) Hood with oreillettes and narrow liripipe. Also peasant's short sleeved kirtle and smock sleeves to wrist. (b) Hood with oreillettes turned back. (c) Draped veil over rising templers. (1428).

5. OUTDOOR GARMENTS

HOODED CLOAKS were still worn for travelling.

Some cloaks were buttoned in front with three or four buttons from chin to chest, and made with high collars to fit over that of the Houppelande, from 1400 to 1410.

6. HEADWEAR

THE HOOD (fourteenth century to 1450, after which continued for homely use, or mourning, to the end of the century). Continued to be worn for travelling and also by humbler folk. Worn open, some with projecting side flaps (Fr. 'oreillettes') standing out like ears from the sides of the face.

Hoods worn by the higher classes were often lined with fur. 'A hood of scarlet cloth and a hood of black cloth, both furred with miniver.'

The *Liripipe,* for women's hoods, had sometimes a peculiar arrangement; being cut vertically it was then turned back and attached down the centre of the back of the hood so that at the bend two small pointed 'horns' projected.

New styles of head wear

During this century very elaborate headgear developed; these styles were thought far more decorative than the hair itself which, with certain exceptions, was not only concealed but often shaved off the forehead.

Breadth was emphasised during the first third of the century; then *height,* until about 1485 when a complete change took place.

The new styles may be classified into *Wide Shapes* and *High Shapes.*

(1) *Wide shape without side pieces (known as Templers or Templettes).*

The Chaplet or 'Cushion' head-dress was a thick padded ring of irregular shape, usually stretched out from side to side; often dagged, and generally trimmed with a jewelled ornament in front, as for men [1380–1410–15]. Worn over a net enclosing the hair, which was coiled above each ear so as to form a rounded knob at each temple. Heavy materials used for winter.

125

55. 15TH CENTURY, 1ST HALF
HEADWEAR

(a) Templers with narrow supporting fillet draped with veil. (1413.)
(b) Side view of templers and veil, also high houppelande collar left
open under chin. (*c.* 1410.) (c) Widow's veil and barbe. (*c.* 1446–50.)

56. 15TH CENTURY, 1ST HALF

Shows the goffering of a veil, draped over pointed templers (rare).
V neck, with revers, of houppelande. (1439.)

'A cap of beaver furred with ermine, garnished with a silk
button and tassel' (Princess Philippa's Trousseau, 1406).

Light materials for other seasons. 'Five silk chaplets' (Princess
Philippa's Trousseau, 1406).

(2) *Wide shapes with Templers or French Templettes*

   (*a*) The ornamental fillet or coronet, sometimes worn over
a net, had reticulated decorative bosses of goldsmith's work,
often jewelled. These bosses enclosing the hair at the temples,
were known as 'Templers' or 'Templettes'. The templettes ended

above the ears until about 1410–15. When pointed to c. 1440 but un-English.

'1 pair of templers 6/8' (Household Accounts of Queen Joan of Navarre 1419–21).

A fine gauze veil often worn under the fillet, directly over the hair, formed a hanging curtain behind [1400–1410–15].

(b) Fillet *with templers extending lower,* completely covering the ears and spreading outwards to a varying extent. The head-piece holding these structures was broadened in proportion, and the whole head-dress became more decorated and elaborate.

Veil optional but usual [1410–1430].

(c) The '*Horned Head-dress*' was an elaboration of (b) worn with a veil which was carried outwards beyond and above the side pieces on wires shaped like cow's horns [1410–1420].

(d) The '*Heart-shaped Head-dress*' was formed by curving the side pieces up into a U over the forehead; the circlet now fitted the temples and was hidden under the side-pieces.

The whole structure was usually draped with a small veil [1420–1450].

(3) *High Shapes*

Worn without projecting side-pieces, and always with a backward tilt.

(a) A *Circular Roll,* sausage-shaped, was bent up on each side into a deep V over the forehead and back of the head. The gap at the sides was filled in now by part of the head covering (where formerly the side-pieces had been placed). The whole structure sat well above the ears with all the hair shaved up to its lower edge. A flowing veil was optional [1440–1480s].

To this type of headgear a gorget and liripipe were occasionally added as a decoration [1445–1460].

(b) A *Turban Head-dress* with an open crown circular or oval in shape, and placed well off the forehead, increased in height as time elapsed. Worn with or without a veil, which was occasionally replaced by the long hair flowing through or under the open top. Not common in England [1440s–1480s].

N.B. A V- or U-shaped loop placed in the centre of the shaved

57. 15TH CENTURY, 1ST HALF

(a) Side view of (b). (b) Wide templers and fillets, with pendant veil behind. (*c.* 1417.) (c) Top view of (b).

a

b

58. 15TH CENTURY, 1ST HALF

(a) Heart-shaped head-dress draped with veil. (Style of 1420–50.)
(b) Fillet with low templers and veil. Houppelande with flat collar.
(1415.)

part of the forehead, was often attached to a high head-dress. Possibly this device was to counter-balance the backward pull of the top-heavy structure.

(4) *Veils*

(*a*) The *old style* of veil continued to be worn domestically and by the elderly and widows throughout the century [1400–1500].

The *Goffered veil* or 'nebula' head-dress also survived for a time [to 1420].

(*b*) The *Wired veil,* draped over the head behind; the straight edge above the forehead was wired to stand out over the hair, which was generally enclosed in a net and dressed to form bosses above the ears.

Sometimes the border across the forehead was ruched or a small jewelled circlet added. As height increased the wiring over the forehead was bent up at each side to form a deep U, similar to that in example (3) (*a*) [1400–1460].

With *thin gauze veils* and *ruched veils* the wiring might be discarded, the veil being loosely draped.

The *Widow's veil.* The veil and wimple together, at this time indicated widowhood, the veil being made of heavy dark material. The wimple, now called the *barbe,* was stitched in vertical pleats and covered the chin when worn by those of high rank; or was worn below the chin by others.

7. HAIR

This was entirely concealed, except for the following, when the hair was worn long and unconfined:

(*a*) By queens at their coronation.

(*b*) By brides, with wreath or fillet (to the seventeenth century).

(*c*) By unmarried girls, until about 1420, and by children.

(*d*) With the open turban.

Shaved foreheads and temples were in fashion, and eyebrow plucking and face painting continued [1370–1480].

a

b

c

59. 15TH CENTURY, 1ST AND 2ND HALF
HEADWEAR

(a) Circular roll raised to form a U over forehead. Sides covered by hair net. (c. 1450–54.) (b) Turban head-dress, the hair brought forward in two plaits fixed to the front instead of hanging loose. (1452.) (c) Horned head-dress with veil wired up over wide templers and surmounted by coronet (1416).

8. FOOTWEAR

(1) SHOES followed the men's fashions, but with shorter points during the piked periods. They were often lined. 'Pair of (shoes) of shaved (i.e. polished) leather furred with backs of greys.'

Punceons or *Pinsons* were thin shoes, possibly slippers, but no contemporary description is known. 'Four pairs of punceons of white leather, two furred with pured miniver, two furred with backs of greys.'

(2) BOOTS were seldom if ever worn.

9. STOCKINGS

Short round hose, gartered above or below the knee.

10. ACCESSORIES

All *Jewellery* as worn by men, including knightly girdles, elaborate necklaces, and SS collars (by Lancastrian ladies of rank).

Also *Pouches,* and occasionally *Daggers.*

Gloves.

Aprons, without bibs, worn domestically.

Elaborate Trimmings, e.g. 'a thousand pearls for embroidering the collar and sleeves of a gown, $16\frac{1}{2}$ oz. of silver-gilt spangs; three tissues of silk' (Princess Philippa's Trousseau, 1406).

Colours: Green and scarlet predominated throughout the period.

Second Half of
the Fifteenth Century

MEN

1. THE DOUBLET

Worn over the shirt. Still close-fitting, well padded, waisted and very short, barely covering the hips.

In 1485 it might end at waist level, without a skirt which was optional at this period.

Fastenings. Down the front by lacing, buttons, ties or hooks and eyes. Eyelet holes for trussing the points still used.

Neck

(*a*) With fairly high stand-up collar having a wide V opening in front [1450–1490], becoming wider and deeper, revealing the shirt, over which the collar was joined by lacing [*c.* 1480s].

(*b*) No collar, but a low square-cut neckline [1490–1530], or sloping to a deep V in front, laced across.

Sleeves

(*a*) Close fitting to wrist, and sometimes detachable, being tied on at armholes [1450–1500].

(*b*) Sometimes slashed across at the elbows, the shirt sleeve bulging through; this was occasionally repeated higher up (1480 to 1500, after which slashing increased).

Materials. Velvet and linen common.

'Doublet of red velvet lined with linen cloth.'

'Doublet of white linen cloth.'

'Item a doublet of crymosyn velvet lined with holland cloth and interlined with busk.' (Inventory of Wardrobe of Edward IV.)

134

60. 15TH CENTURY, 2ND HALF

(a) Joined hose and waistcoat. Points giving way. (1450–60.) (b) Short doublet laced across stomacher. Shirt showing at neck and through slashed sleeve. Long hose. Codpiece. Typical shoes. Round cap. (1479–87.) (c) Doublet with sleeves slashed across at elbow. (Style of 1480–1500.) (d) Jacket laced across doublet, hanging sleeves with emerging doublet sleeves. Round cap, and beaver hat slung over shoulder by attached liripipe. Short boots. (1479–87.) (e) Doublet with detachable sleeves. Long buskins with turn over tops. Plumed beaver hat. (1490–1500.)

'Buske' was also mentioned as a padding for Richard III's doublet in 1483 [MS. Harl No. 4780].

2. THE PETTICOAT or WAISTCOAT [1450s–1515]

A short garment, worn for warmth, under the doublet and over the shirt. Usually padded. Tight fitting, with or without tight fitting sleeves. Round neck, usually lower at the back.

'One petticoat of linen cloth stuffed with flock.'

'One petticoat of linen without sleeves' (Sir John Fastolf's Wardrobe Accounts, 1459).

3. THE JACKET (1450 to 1660, but after 1500 usually called Jerkin). Replacing the Cote-hardie. Worn over the doublet, which was always concealed by it at the hem.

Length

(a) To mid-thigh, sometimes with side vents.

(b) Barely covering the hips, and increasingly uncovering the seat.

Shape. Tight fitting and well waisted, with a narrow belt from which its skirt flared out with some fulness when made in the longer style [1450–1480].

(a) Fashionable form, with vertical folds front and back radiating fan-wise up and down from the centre of the waist; the sides smooth and plain.

(b) Unfashionable form, plain well-fitting body with full skirt falling in loose folds.

A later style of jacket with formal gathers, longer skirts often made separately from the body and known as '*bases*', was commoner in the sixteenth century [1480–1540. Bases ended *c.* 1540].

'A doublet of blac satyn made and lyned accordingly with a base of a jacket and a stomacher both of blac satyn' [Wardrobe Accounts of Edward IV].

Mahoitres [1450–1480s] were shoulder pads over which the sleeves were gathered to the shoulder seam. This was a device for producing the characteristic broad shoulders of jackets and gowns.

The Neck

(a) No collar, but a round neck with a short wide V opening

a   b

61. 15TH CENTURY, 2ND HALF

(a) Jacket with low neck line revealing doublet collar. Loose open
sleeves. Shoes very pointed. Chaperon. (1460's.) (b) Fur-trimmed
jacket with hanging sleeve. Doublet sleeve emerging. Small plumed
cap. Piked shoes. (c. 1470–80.)

62. 15TH CENTURY, 2ND HALF

(a) Jacket trimmed with fur. Doublet collar showing above. Pointed pattens with dark shoes. Chaperon with long liripipe. (c. 1456.) (b) (c) Jackets with vertically slashed sleeves showing doublet sleeve which in (c) is also slashed showing shirt sleeve. (c. 1470.)

138

in front or behind, or a narrow V in front to waist [1450–1480s].

(*b*) A deep V opening in front, the point reaching the waist and revealing the doublet, or a separate chest piece called a 'stomacher', which barely extended below the waist [1480s–1490s].

'Warme your soverayne his petticotte, his doublett and his stomacher . . .' (Boke of Karvyng, late fifteenth century).

Sleeves

(1) Closed

(*a*) Full above, narrowing to the wrist, without gathers, and there buttoned.

(*b*) Full and gathered into a buttoned wristband. Such sleeves often had a vertical slash generally laced across and revealing the underlying doublet or shirt sleeve.

(2) Open

Full above, tubular, narrowing slightly to the wrist and often rolled back to the elbow, thus producing a short sleeve. The lining gave the appearance of a wide cuff.

(3) Hanging sleeves ('Side sleeves surplice-wise', 'side' or 'syde' meaning 'wide').

Open in the form of a wide tube hanging to the knees or lower; often the two were tied together behind to keep them out of the way.

The usual upper slit for the arm was fairly deep.

Materials

Velvet, chamlet, figured satin (the last forbidden to all below rank of knight, by Sumptuary Law of Edward IV), fustian and leather.

Linings of linen or blanket cloth. (Where some of the garment was likely to be hidden by the gown, this might be made of inferior material. See Example (*c*).)

Examples (From Wardrobe Accounts of Sir J. Fastolf, d. 1459).

(*a*) 'Jacket of blue velvet lined in the body with small linen cloth and the sleeves with blanket.'

(*b*) 'Jacket of red velvet, the vents bound with red leather.'

a

b

c

63. 15TH CENTURY, 2ND HALF

(a) Hooded cape. (*c.* 1458–9.) (b) Long gown, shoulders broadened over mahoitres, and low V neck behind. Chaperon. Piked shoes. (*c.* 1460–70.) (c) Long gown, hanging sleeves, one worn normally. Hat with attached liripipe draped over shoulder. (*c.* 1460–70.)

64. 15TH CENTURY, 2ND HALF

(a) Large plumed hat (p. 150 (3) h) worn over undercap. Demi-gown, without belt; long hanging sleeves. Coarse over-stockings and broad shoes. (*c.* 1490–1500.) (b) Long ceremonial gown. Small 'pork pie' cap. (*c.* 1494.)

(*c*) 'Jacket, the breast and sleeves of black velvet, the rest of russet fustian.'

(*d*) 'Jacket of deer's leather, neck edged with black velvet.'

The COAT at this period has not been identified, but was probably a synonym for jacket.

'A clene sherte and breche, a petticote, a doublett, a long cotte, a stomacher, hys socks and hys schone' were the clothes prepared for a man to dress himself in (Boke of Curtasye).

4. THE GOWN (Previously called the Houppelande)

Continued to be made on the same principle as formerly, ground length or knee length with no vents.

The pleats, arranged like massed organ pipes in front and behind for the whole length, were stitched into place at the waist under the belt, the sides being plain.

Fastened all down the front by hooks and eyes or sometimes made double-breasted.

Mahoitres to broaden the shoulders were characteristic.

Neck

(1) The short upright collar with rounded or blunt corners sloping to a V in front continued for a few years [1425–1460].

(2) No collar

    (*a*) Round neck [1425–1500]

    (*b*) With V at the back [1430–1480s]

    (*c*) With U at the back [1450–1470]

    (*d*) With V in front [1430–1465]

(3) A flat square-cut collar at the back, continued forward over the shoulders in long broad revers, sometimes reaching down to the hem in front; often faced with fur [1485–1540].

Belt optional during last quarter of century, the gown being:

    (*a*) Tied at the waist by a narrow girdle, or

    (*b*) Allowed to hang loosely without a belt, the front left open. When short, known as a demi-gown.

Sleeves

(1) Open. Plain and cylindrical to wrist, or ceremonially, wide at wrist, sometimes rolled up to make a short sleeve. Not very common [1415–1485].

(2) Closed. Usually very full; plain or gathered at the shoulder, and shaped to the wrist without a band, or gathered into a wristband. Any combination of these allowable [1405–1500].

(3) Hanging, 'surplice-wise'. Of the open cylindrical type with large upper opening down the front seam, for the arm [1430–1625].

Fur borders continued.

Linings usual, but not invariable.

Materials (from Household Accounts of Sir John Fastolf):—

65. 15TH CENTURY, 2ND HALF

Gown with stand-up collar sloping to a V in front. Very full sleeves. Slightly modified 'bowl crop'. (*c.* 1450–60.)

'Gown of cloth of gold with side-sleeves surplice-wise.'
'Gown of blue velvet upon velvet, furred with marten, and purfled (i.e. edged) of the same.'
'Gown of cloth of green.'
'One side scarlet gown, not lined.'
'One red gown leveret-lined.'
'Gown of French russet lined with black cloth.'

5. THE HUKE [1455–1480]

Very rare except for the *pedestrian tabard*. Ground length. The front and back panels were either (*a*) Bound to the waist by a girdle, or

(*b*) The front panel alone was secured by the girdle, the back panel falling loose like a cloak.

Some hukes had sleeves, and were trimmed with fur; some were dagged. 'One jagged huke of black sengle' (Wardrobe Accounts of Sir John Fastolf, 1459).

CEREMONIAL MANTLES continued.

6. CLOAKS

Very rare; used for extra warmth and for travelling.

Capes, thigh length and sometimes hooded, occasionally worn.

7. HOSE

Continued as 'tights', gradually extending higher until the waist was reached (*c.* 1475).

The 'breech' was the name given to the portion covering the seat. This was sometimes of a different colour and even different material from the legs [*c.* 1485]. It was often decorated with small puffs, embroidery, or with a network of crossed bands [*c.* 1490].

Parti-coloured hose returned to fashion in 1485. Striped hose were also popular.

Trussing of hose continued, either to the doublet or to the 'waistcoat'.

The *Codpiece* remained in fashion.

Over-stockings, thick, and loosely fitting, and turned down with a broad fold at the knee, were sometimes worn. The *shape* of the feet as for shoes and boots.

Separate hose still worn by labourers.

8. FOOTWEAR

(1) BOOTS OR BUSKINS. Long, well up the thigh and loose or fitting the leg and laced up on the inner or outer side; far more popular now than during the first half of the century. Used for riding and walking. Deep turned-over tops were common [1450–1500].

66. 15TH CENTURY, 2ND HALF

(a) Short jacket. Long buskins with turn-over tops. Plumed hat.
(c. 1460.) (b) Hose attached by points to doublet. (c. 1460.) (c) Peasants'
hose with stirrup feet. Codpiece. Large hat. (d) Doublet sleeve slashed
at elbow. Thick over-stockings turned down below knees, and over-
shoes. (1480–1500.) (e) Jacket with hanging sleeve. Slippers. (c. 1468.)

67. 15TH CENTURY, 2ND HALF
FOOTWEAR

(a) Shoes and boots with long points, piked. (Style of 1460–80.)
(b) Late leather pattens. (1498–99.) (c) Piked shoe with wooden patten
of very simple design. (d) Short buskins. (1498–99.)

Short buskins continued in use.

Shape of foot

(*a*) Short points [1450–1460].

(*b*) Piked [1460–1480].

(*c*) Shorter points [1480–1490].

(*d*) Duck-billed, i.e. square with rounded corners becoming splayed towards 1510 [1490–1515].

(2) SHOES

Some continued with the high cut round the ankle, but most adopted the new style which was characteristic; cut with a deep V on both sides, leaving a long pointed tongue in front of the ankle, and a similar flap rising up behind the ankle.

Slippers with open tops occurred, but were uncommon.

(3) PATTENS. These continued, their most fashionable period being from 1440–1460.

(4) SLOPPES [1481]. A kind of shoe mentioned in inventory of Edward IV. Made of blue, red and tawny Spanish leather; some lined with black velvet, others unlined. 'A pair of slops of black leather at 18d a pair' was one of the payments to the king's shoe-maker.

Possibly an overshoe, such as a pantofle (or mule) mentioned in 1496 (Linthicum).

N.B. The name was also applied to a mourning garment shaped like a cassock, e.g. 'A duke, for his gown, slope and mantille, 16 yards at 10/- the yard'.

9. HEAD WEAR

(1) The HOOD was worn occasionally for a few years, especially on horseback. '1 rydyng hode of rede felwet with iiii jagys' (Ward-robe Accounts of Sir John Fastolf, 1459).

(2) THE CHAPERON continued until *c.* 1470, and longer with the elderly and peasants.

(3) HATS

(*a*) Large crown with flat or rounded top, and broad or narrow brim turned up or down [1450–1480s].

(*b*) Round crown ('bowler' style), the brim rolled or closely turned up or down. Commonly trimmed with upright feather

68. 15TH CENTURY, 2ND HALF

(a) Piked patten without and with shoe, showing raised sole and heel.
(b) Pattens worn.

a

b

69. 15TH CENTURY, 2ND HALF

(a) Small round cap, close turned-up brim, and jewelled ornament. Hair style (p. 115 10 (c)). (Style 1475–1500.) (b) Tall cap with stalk. (1462.)

in front or behind, and attached by jewelled ornament [1400–1500].

(*c*) Tall tapering crown with rolled brim or none [1445–1485].

(*d*) Tall tapering crown with brim peaked in front and turned up behind, a variation of similar styles in previous period and fourteenth century [1430–1460].

(*e*) Large ballooned crown [1430–1460].

(*f*) Plain beaver with moderate crown and brim; attached liripipe for slinging the hat over the shoulder. Frequently carried in this way when another style was being worn [1445–1500].

(*g*) Straw hats of various simple shapes.

(*h*) Large upturned bowl-shaped brim with low crown and large plume of ostrich feathers sometimes spangled. Worn at the back of the head, or slung by strings on the shoulder [1490s–1505].

(4) CAPS known as *bonnets*

(*a*) Felt cap resembling a Turkish fez, varying in height, with and without a stalk [1450–1485].

(*b*) Flat 'pork-pie' cap, close turned up brim and jewelled ornament [1475–1500].

(*c*) A round cap with flat or slightly raised crown and brim closely turned up, but with a gap in front sometimes laced across with gold or silver cords [1480–1515].

10. HAIR (N.B. descriptive terms only)

(*a*) The *Bowl crop* [1410–1460].

(*b*) The *modified bowl crop,* similar, but with the hair longer, partly covering the forehead, ears and back of neck [1450–1475].

(*c*) The '*Page boy*' *cut*. A forehead fringe, curly or straight; or a centre parting. The rest of the hair hanging down to the neck or sometimes to the shoulders, and frequently waved [1465–1515].

Face generally clean-shaven.

70. 15TH CENTURY, 2ND HALF

(a) Modified 'bowl crop' hair style. (1483—a late survival.) (b) Hat
with large crown and turned up brim. (p. 147 3 (a)). Also shows furred
neck of gown and doublet collar above. (c. 1450.)

11. ACCESSORIES

As for the first half of the fifteenth century. Heavy *jewelled necklaces* were very prevalent.

Handkerchiefs, called '*Handcoverchiefs*' are mentioned in the Wardrobe Accounts of Edward IV.

Breast coverchiefs were worn over the shirt at breast level. Mentioned as being made of holland in Edward IV's wardrobe, 1480.

Muckinder or Mokador (a vulgar term), was a common person's or child's handkerchief or linen square used as a table napkin. 'For eyen and nose, the nedeth a mokadow' (Lydgate's 'Advice to an Old Gentleman who wished for a Young Wife').

Gloves. 'The manufacture must have been adequate for home needs by 1463; in that year King Edward forbade the importation of gloves into England' (Linthicum).

Pouches, sometimes called 'Pokes', corresponding to detachable pockets. '1 russet poke' (Wardrobe Accounts of Sir John Fastolf).

Second Half of the Fifteenth Century

WOMEN

1. THE KIRTLE

Continued in use but was rarely visible. If worn uncovered, this was an act of penance.

2. THE GOWN.

Previously called the *Houppelande*.

Worn over the Kirtle, and now women's principle upper garment. Its styles changed rapidly between 1450 and 1460, the old and new forms overlapping.

NEW STYLE 1 [1450–1480s]

The formal tubular folds were discarded, and the skirt fell in loose flowing lines from the fairly high waist to a very ample width on the ground. Long trains were common.

(1) *The Bodice,* comfortably fitting and gathered into the waist, had a V neck edged with revers as formerly, but at the back the V was not always carried downwards, the collar curving low round the neck.

The Bodice became closer fitting; the revers tended to be placed further off the shoulders, baring the neck, which was cut low in front with a curved or straight edge; the revers being brought down in an open V to the waist, or continued under the belt to a level lower still.

The collar was frequently furred, and always matched the cuffs.

The wide V opening was often laced across the kirtle bodice, or

71. 15TH CENTURY, 2ND HALF

(a) Old style gown, fur trimmed, held up and showing embroidered hem of kirtle. Pointed shoe. Butterfly head-dress. (1448, but head-dress corresponding to English 1450.) (b) (c) Leather pattens.

occasionally over an ornamental 'fill-in' called a *stomacher*. Only very rarely was the V opening not edged with a collar.

(2) *Sleeves*. Three types:

(*a*) Immense funnel-shapes, with the lower end of the wide aperture falling towards the hem [1450–1460s].

(*b*) Loose fitting and cylindrical to the wrist, usually cuffed or edged with fur [1450–1470s].

(*c*) Tight fitting, ending at the wrist in either a large turned-back cuff or a mitten-like prolongation to the knuckles [1460–1520].

(Both were probably the same cuff turned up or down.)

Mahoitres were not worn by women.

(3) *The Belt*

Usually very broad; often embroidered; worn at a high waist level, well pulled in.

NEW STYLE II [1470s–1500]

The *bodice* moulded the figure to the waist and, more often, to hip level; there the expanding skirt hung in natural folds of full drapery to the ground; long trains were frequent.

Fastened by almost invisible lacing in front, or sometimes behind.

A seam at the waist joining bodice and skirt began to appear, *c*. 1470, in the construction of gowns.

Occasionally this gown ended just below the knee, acting like a surcoat over the kirtle which swept the ground.

The Neck line was very low, the front edge often curving up into a short point at the centre.

A flat falling collar of the 'bertha' type, frequently of fur, and always matching the cuffs, bordered the neck line, widening out over the shoulders; and passing below the upcurved point in the centre front.

Sleeves. Of the type (*c*) previously described.

The Belt was narrow, usually composed of ornamental metal plaques, and worn loosely round the waist, or more often at hip level; usually finished with a long hanging end.

Occasionally absent.

b

a

c

72. 15TH CENTURY, 2ND HALF

(a) Gown style I (p. 153) with high crowned 'bonnet' head-dress.
(c. 1460–90.) (b) Gown style II (p. 155) with similar head-dress. Lower
crown. (1490.) (c) Gown style III (p. 157) and turban head-dress.
(1479–857.)

My narrow gilt girdle and enamelled girdle of velvet upon satin' (Will of Margaret Odeham of Bury 1492).

'A girdle of black harnessed with silver gilt and enamelled' (M. Paston. *Norfolk Archaeological Journal*, Vol. III).

In all low-necked gowns a 'fill-in', called a gorget, of folds of a soft white material, crossing the shoulders to a V front and back, was often worn. Alternatively, very large and elaborate necklaces or neck collars were extremely fashionable.

NEW STYLE III

A variation of Style II, and very uncommon in England. The line of the tight-fitting bodice was broken by pleats or gathers stitched down at the centre of the neck edge, front and back, and then allowed to flow free and loose to the ground.

Usually *no belt* was worn.

The *Neck* was moderately low, widening to the shoulders. The *bertha* was shaped in a wide oval, often overlapping the shoulders. When omitted it was replaced by a stitched-down narrow band of material.

The *sleeves* were of the type (2) (*c*) previously described; or, less commonly, *hanging sleeves,* open from above the elbow, the pendant parts forming a broad tippet of ankle length; or tight to the elbow, the kirtle sleeve carried on to the wrist.

NEW STYLE IV [from 1495]

At the close of the century there appeared a loose gown with a square neck, above which might appear the top of the kirtle or the folds of the gorget (or fill-in). This gown was fastened invisibly down the front. An alternate bodice was laced across a wide V opening in front, and both styles might be similarly laced behind.

Occasionally the gown hung loose from the shoulders, but usually the bodice was close fitting.

The skirt was always full and trained.

Such gowns could be worn alone, or over the close-fitting kirtle as described. The train was long, and often turned up and fastened to the belt behind, or if no belt was worn it was pinned with a brooch or tied up at this level, or draped over one arm. Thus the lining of rich material was displayed.

a

b

73. 15TH CENTURY, 2ND HALF

(a) Gown style IV (p. 157). Low hood-like head-dress (1495–1500).
(b) Gown style IV with train turned up showing fur lining. Back
lacing to bodice. Low hood with front border turned back and showing
under cap. (c. 1495–1500.)

74. 15TH CENTURY, 2ND HALF
HEADWEAR

(a) (c) Variations of high V-shaped roll with attached ornamenta
gorget and liripipe. (c. 1450–60.) (b) Truncated cone-shaped head-dress
with flowing veil. (c. 1480.) (d) High crowned bonnet shaped head
dress with V loop over forehead. (c. 1484.)

75. 15TH CENTURY, 2ND HALF
The 'Chimney pot' head-dress with narrow veil looped round chin.

The *sleeves* were usually large, and very wide at the wrists (this style of gown developed into the characteristic garment of the Tudor period in the next century).

Lining and Trimming of Gowns

The use of fur was still very prevalent.

'A long gown of fine crimson (or green) velvet furred with miniver and purfled (edged) with ermine' [1465].

'Long gown of black velvet furred with marten and purfled with ermine.'

'A long gown of violet engrained, furred and purfled with marten' (Sir John Howard's gifts to his wife, Stoke-by-Nayland).

3. THE SIDELESS SURCOAT [1360–1500, and as state apparel up to 1520].

Continued in use, but towards the close of the century it tended to become a ceremonial garment only.

4. MANTLES

These remained unchanged.

'A mantle of white cloth of gold damaske, furred with ermine fastened on her breast with a large lace (cord) curiously wrought with gold and silk with rich knoppes (tassels) of gold at the end tasselled', was worn by Elizabeth of York, Queen of Henry VII, on the day of her coronation (Cotton MS. Julius B XII).

5. HEADWEAR

During the second half of the fifteenth century up to 1485–90, all head-dresses were tall, placed high on the head, and worn with a backward tilt.

The hair was shaved up to the lower margin of the tight-fitting headgear, and the ears, with rare exceptions, were left uncovered.

The U loop on the forehead was conspicuous.

Types:

(a) The 'Sausage-shaped' Roll, with deep V over the forehead, described previously, continued, though it was usually more elongated [1440–1485].

(b) A similar shape with the U over the forehead, but the substructure entirely concealed by a thick veil [1440–1485].

(c) The turban head-dress, increasing in size and height [1440–1485].

(d) The 'chimney-pot' head-dress, so shaped, with a veil attached to the top and allowed to flow behind. Rarely a gorget and liripipe attached instead [1460–1480s].

(e) The 'truncated cone' was the English modification of the French 'hennin' or steeple-shaped head-dress, the latter being avoided in this country. The cone had the shape of an inverted flower-pot, and was draped with a large gauze veil; this flowed down freely behind, and was sometimes so long that it had to be carried over the arm [1460–1480].

(f) The 'High-crowned Bonnet'. In this the crown varied

a

b

c

76. 15TH CENTURY, 2ND HALF
HEADWEAR

(a) Butterfly headdress pinned up over side pieces (rare in England). (1449.) (b) Veil draped in a U over high side pieces. (1458). (c) Butterfly headdress showing hair strained back into the usual supporting cap. Top of gown style II. Elaborate necklace. (1482.)

a

b

77. 15TH CENTURY, 2ND HALF

(a) Butterfly headdress of transparent gauze arranged low over forehead. (Style of 1450–85.) (b) Plain linen hood (c. 1480's). (Style of
1485–1500.) (Both these headdresses appeared earlier abroad.)

from a short truncated cone to a much lower shape, either flat-topped or sometimes domed. A broad turned-back brim curved round the face and descended stiffly on each side to the shoulders [1460–1490s].

(g) The 'Butterfly Head-dress'. Very characteristic of nearly the whole of the second half of the fifteenth century, surviving all other forms, though infrequent after 1485.

Consisted of a large gauze veil supported on a wire frame, with the usual V dip over the forehead. The whole structure presented the appearance of a pair of diaphanous 'wings' spreading out above the head. It was built up on a small ornamental cap in the shape of a fez, which was worn on the back of the head enclosing all the hair.

Sometimes a transparent fold of gauze was stretched low over the forehead, perhaps to check the head-dress from slipping backwards [1450–1495].

After 1485 and the end of the Yorkist dynasty, a sudden change (coinciding with the new Tudor dynasty) appeared in women's headgear.

Only the 'high crowned hood' and the 'butterfly' head-dresses survived, and these not after 1495.

The new mode appearing from 1485 (and continuing into the sixteenth century) was a low hoodlike covering, worn similarly to the old-fashioned veil, its straight edge framing the face, with the material draped back over the head and falling outwards to the shoulders. This hood was lined with some bright contrasting colour; and the broad fold which was turned back round the face gave a decorative 'surround' and exposed a close-fitting under cap. This was shaped like a coif, and was usually tied under the chin, being made of linen, or velvet often edged with a jewelled embroidery. (From this developed the English 'Gable head-dress' of the sixteenth century.)

A similar hood of plain linen, with a stiffened edge framing the face, fell in ample folds to the shoulders and neck.

78. 15TH CENTURY, 2ND HALF

(a) Simple caul (*c.* 1490–1500). (b) Gown style IV with hood and undercap. (*c.* 1495–1500.) (c) Beck worn by young girl with flowing hair. (1495 on.)

INDOOR HEADWEAR

(*a*) *The Crespin* was an ornamental hair net edged with a jewelled turban-like roll.

(*b*) *The Caul* was a close-fitting coif-like head-dress covering the ears; reticulated in gold thread decorated with jewels or pearls, and sometimes lined with taffeta or tissue. When worn with a fillet or coronet it was very like styles at the end of the fourteenth century.

The Beck was a beak-like piece of material worn point forwards above the centre of the forehead; by young girls it was pinned to the hair, by married women fastened under the head-dress. The fashion was not very popular or approved of by authority. Thus, in the 'Order for wearing of Aparelle' at the funeral of Henry VII's mother in 1493, it was directed 'that in no manner of wise beakes be used, for the deformity of the same' (Strutt).

Frontlets were forehead bands worn across the forehead usually with a veil and made of cloth, silk, velvet or gold (Privy Purse Expenses of Elizabeth of York).

MOURNING APPAREL

The *Hood*, of the old-fashioned type, but with modifications, was worn for mourning.

Thus in the above-mentioned Order—'A duchess to weare a playne hood without clokes, and tippette (i.e. liripipe) at the hoode, in length to the grounde and in breadth a nayle and a half an inche; Lordes daughters and Knightes wives to wear their hoodes with clokes; and tippettes in breadth three quarters of a nayle, and in length a yard and a half, to be pynned upon their arme.

'The Queenes gentlewomen to weare hoodes and clokes, the tippettes a yarde longe and an inch broad, to be pynned on the sydes of their hoodes. All chamberers shall wear hoodes with clokes and no manner of tippettes. Great estates wearing mantelles, when they ride, to have short clokes and hoodes, with narrow tippettes, to be bound about their heades; and alone as they come to court they to laye away their hoodes; and that after the first month none to weare hoodes in their betters presence, but when they labour.'

79. 15TH CENTURY, 2ND HALF
Elaborate jewelled caul worn with coronet. (1498–99.)

A slope 'is a mourning cassock for ladies and gentlewomen not open before' ('The Manners and Customs of the English' Joseph Strutt).

The *Circotte* 'is a mourning garment, made like a strayte-bodied gowne, wore under a mantle'.

'A Marquesse to weare a surcote with a trayne before and another behynde, a mantle with a trayne. . . . The Queenes gentlewomen to weare sloppes or cot harders' (cote-hardies).

167

6. HAIR

This was completely concealed, or occasionally seen strained back from the forehead when the head-dress was worn very far back and shaving was incomplete.

Face-painting and eyebrow plucking continued in fashion. (To c. 1480.)

7. STOCKINGS or Hose as in the first half of the century.

But those of the poorer classes were still made of coarse wool.

> She hobbles as she goes
> With her blanket hose.
>
>   (Skelton)

8. FOOTWEAR

SHOES as for men, but never piked.

BUSKINS worn for travelling; e.g. For two pair of buskins for the Queen's Grace at her departing into Wales (Privy Purse Expenses of Elizabeth of York).

PATTENS had short pointed toes with cross straps over the instep, placed well forward; no heel support. These were often worn directly over the hose.

9. ACCESSORIES

As in the first half of the century.

Belts and *Girdles* were very elaborate.

'A little girdle of cloth of gold; another of green damask' [1465]. 'A little girdle of silk and gold called a damasent' [1465]. Sir John Howard's gifts to his wife, Stoke by Nayland. The demiceint had front half of goldsmith's work, back half plain silk.

Glossary

OF MATERIALS, COLOURS, AND TERMS OF MULTIPLE OR UNCERTAIN MEANING NOT DEFINED IN THE TEXT

(*N.B.*—The mediaeval spelling was, of course, very variable, the same word often appearing in different forms.)

AGLET, AIGULET or AIGLET. The metal tag to a lace (called a point).

AULMONIERE or ALNER. A purse.

BALANDRANA. A wide cloak for travellers, twelfth and thirteenth centuries.

BARME CLOTH. Apron (Chaucer).

BASELARD. A long dagger worn by civilians (see John Torell's Will) [1400].

BAUDEKIN. Silk cloth with warp of gold thread.

BESSHE. The skin of a doe (?) 'A gown furred with Besshe' [1422].

BETEN. Embroidered with fancy subjects.

BEVER. Beaver.

BICE. Skin of female deer.

BIRRUS or BUREL. A thick rough woollen cloth.

BISS or BISSYN. Fine linen.

BLIAUT. French term for (*a*) Costly material. (*b*) A man's costume worn with armour or at court. (*c*) A lady's Court dress (eleventh and twelfth centuries, see Goddard for quotations).

BOTEWS. Corresponded to buskins 'Pair Botews of blac leder above the Kne . . . paire botews sengle blac ledre with the knee' (Wardrobe Accounts of Edward IV) [1480].

BRANCHED VELVET. Figured velvet.

BROCHED CLOTH. Cloth worked with words or ornaments of gold upon it.

BROELLA. A coarse cloth.

BROWNESWYKE. A kind of linen cloth probably made at Brunswick.

BUDGE or BOGEY. Lambskin with the fur dressed outwards.

BURNET. A cloth of brown colour. Thirteenth century.

BYSSINE. A fine cotton or flax material. Thirteenth century.

CADACE. Flock for padding garments.

CADDIS or CRUEL. A worsted mixed with wool.

CAMELINE. An imported cashmere.

CAURI-MAURY. A coarse rough textile.

CAMLET or CHAMLETT. A stuff of wool and goat's hair.

CAPA PLUVIALIS or CHAPE À PLUIE. A large cloak to protect against rain.

CAMISIA. Shirt or smock.

CAMOCA. A rich silk fabric, rare in England.

CANVAS. A textile of hemp or of coarse linen.

CELESTINE. A light blue form of Plunket.

CENDAL. A silk textile resembling a coarse Sarcenet.

CHAISEL. A fine linen for smocks.

CHALON. A cloth or garment frysed on both sides (Chaucer).

CHAMMER. A jacket with chequered open-work pattern.

CHAMPEYN. A fine linen cloth. Fifteenth century.

CHEKLATON. A costly silk embroidered in chequered knots.

CHELE. Fur from the marten's throat.

CIRCLET. A metal fillet worn by ranks below the nobility.

CLOT SHOEN. Shoes shod with thin iron plates.

COAT or COTE. The term 'cote' occurs in French literature as early as 1159 (Goddard), and by the thirteenth century was common both in England and on the Continent, being apparently identical with tunic. It represents a simple type of everyday dress worn by both sexes and all classes. The word was rarely used for women's attire after the 1420s, and even previously gown or kirtle was more usual. Not until the sixteenth century did cote or coat begin to take on the modern meaning of an outer garment.

COCKERS. High laced boots worn by countrymen ('Piers Plowman').

COGWARE. A coarse common cloth resembling frieze.

COUCHED. Trimmed (Chaucer).

COURTEPY. A short cloak of coarse cloth (Chaucer).

CRACOWES. Long-toed boots or shoes. Fourteenth century.

CREMYLL. Cotton openwork or lace. Fourteenth century.

CUT WORK. In the fourteenth and fifteenth centuries signified the cutting of the borders of garments into fanciful shapes, i.e. 'dagging'. In the sixteenth century it was a special kind of lace.

CYCLAS. A rich stuff of purple colour, imported.

DEMYSENT. A half girdle. Only front half ornamental. Fifteenth century.

DORELET. A hairnet embroidered with jewels.

ENBRAUDE. Embroidered.

ENBRAUDEN. Embroider.

ENGREYNEN. To dye in grain (dyed in the thread before weaving).

FALDING. A coarse cloth resembling Frieze (Chaucer).

FALWE. Yellow.

FERRET-SILKE. Coarse silk.

FLURT-SILKE. Figured silk.

FOYNES. Skin of Polecat.

FRIEZE. A napped rough cloth.

FRONTLET. A forehead band of cloth, silk, or velvet. Fifteenth century.

FROUNCE. The modern flounce. Fourteenth century.

FUNES or FOYNES. Marten skins.

FUSTIAN. A coarse twilled cloth of cotton; also of wool.

FYCHEUX. Fur of the Foumart, 'otherwise called the Polecat or Fichet' [1418].

GAZZATUM. A fine silk or linen gauze. Thirteenth century.

GENETS. See Ionetis.

GIPCIERE. A pouch or purse.

GIRDELSTEDE. The waist (Saxon).

GITE. A gown (Chaucer).

GRISE. A grey fur of Russian squirrel.

HANSELINES. Not identified, but probably a jacket. 'Cut slops or hanselines' condemned by the Parson in Chaucer's 'Canterbury Tales' were obviously garments made too short.

HATERE. Attire.

HERYGOUD. A cloak with hanging sleeves (temp. Edward II).

HOLLAND CLOTH. A linen cloth.

HOWVE. A hood (Chaucer). Or cap (Saxon).

HURE. A cap. Thirteenth and fourteenth centuries.

INDE. Azure-coloured.

IONETIS. The genet, the fur of which resembles the marten's.

JORNADE. A kind of cloak.

KENDAL. A coarse green cloth.

KENNEL. The triangular head-dress for women, end of fifteenth century.

KERSCHE. Kerchief.

KERSEY. A double-twilled Say.

KIRTLE. Of Saxon origin, and most commonly used as given in the text. But it was a 'term which has been applied, at different periods, to nearly every imaginable garment worn by male or female in these islands—a petticoat, safeguard . . . long mantle . . . an apron, a jacket and a loose gown' (Planché 'Cyclopaedia of Costume').

KNOP. A button (Piers Plowman). Also a tassel.

KOURTE-BY. See Courtepy.

LACE. Before the sixteenth century signified a small cord or tie, e.g. shoe lace. 'Drew a lace of silk full clere; adowne then fell his mantyll' (Harl MS. 2252).

LACH. Cloak or mantle (Saxon).

LAKE. A fine lawn (Chaucer).

LETTICE. A fur resembling Ermine.

LIBBARD. Leopard green gown furred with libbards. Will of John Ryngfeld [1439].

MARTRONS. Martens. 'The most beautiful of all the Weasel kind.'

MUSTERDEVILLIS. 'A kind of mixed grey woollen cloth' (Halliwell). 'Probably Mestier de Velours, a half velvet' (Fenn). Possibly also a colour (mustard).

NIFLES. A sort of veil. Fifteenth century.

NOUCH or **OUCH.** A jewelled clasp or buckle (Chaucer).

PALTOCK. Some kind of a jacket or gipon, of Spanish origin, and introduced into England during the reign of Edward III.

PAMPILION. A fur.

PELLARD. A garment resembling a super-tunic.

PEPLUS. A large coverchief or veil, twelfth century. Later a very large shawl-like mantle used by men.

PELURIN. Purfled or edged with fur.

PERSE. A bluish grey. Also a material.

PILION. A round hat (Piers Plowman).

PILCHE. A coat or cloak of skins or fur. In Henry V's wardrobe after his death there were two pilches of 'crist-gray' fur.

PLUNKET. A coloured cloth, originally of fine quality.

POINTS. Ties for attaching hose, as described in the text. They were originally the metal tags on thongs of leather, but the term was transferred to the thongs when the tags were called by the French name aiguilette—anglicised to Aglet.

PONGE. A purse (Chaucer).

PONYET. A cuff of a sleeve, fifteenth century.

POPLE. Fur from the back of a squirrel, fifteenth century.

POULAINES. Long-pointed shoes or boots.

POUNSONED. Punched with a bodkin.

POWDERED. Sprinkled over, e.g. 'A pair of vestments of white damask, powdered with bears and ragged staves of gold.' Will of Elizabeth Lady Latimer [1480].

PRANKEN. To arrange the folds of a gown.

PUKE. The colour puce; also a stuff commonly used for making hose and gowns.

PURFLE. A border of trimming.

RAISED GOWN. One with a new nap set on the material.

RAY. A striped cloth, fourteenth century.

RAYNES. A fine linen, originally from Rennes.

RENO. A short mantle of precious furs, possible hooded (Norman).

ROKETTE. A woman's loose upper garment (Chaucer).

ROSKYN. Fur of the squirrel in summer.

RULLIONS. A rough kind of shoe, fifteenth century.

RUSSET. A dark brown colour; also a coarse cloth.

SAMITE. A very rich silk often interwoven with gold thread.

SANGUINE. Scarlet.

SATIN FUGRE. Figured satin.

SARCIATUS or SARZIL. A coarse woollen cloth.

SAY. A woollen cloth, sometimes a silk textile.

SCHAWERE. A veil.

SCLAVYN. A pilgrim's mantle.

SEINT or SEYNT. A Girdle.

SICLATON. Same as Baudekin, thirteenth century.

SIDE GOWN. Wide gown.

SINDON. A fine linen cloth.

SINGLE GOWN. An unlined gown.

SLOPPES. ? A jacket in the fourteenth century.
   Shoes or a cassock in the fifteenth century.
   Breeches in the sixteenth century.
   'Slops ... have been "everything by turns" and certainly "nothing long" ..., and the name is now most appropriately assigned to slop-sellers, who are dealers in all sorts of old clothes' (Planché, 1876).

SPANG. A metal fastening.

STAMEL. A kind of fine worsted, generally red.

STAMFORTIS. A strong and costly cloth (Anglo-Norman).

STAMIN. A slight woollen stuff. Or a worsted of a coarse kind.

SEQUANIE or SOSQUENIE.
SUKKENYE. } A loose frock worn over their other clothes by countrywomen (Chaucer)
SUPERTOTUS.

TACHE. A clasp.

TARTARYN. A costly mediaeval stuff, the nature unknown.

TAVESTOCKE. A Broadcloth.

TAWNY. A dusky brown-orange colour.

TEMPLYS. Templettes (French). 'My grete templys with the baleys (pale rubies).' Will of Countess of Warwick [1439].

TIPPET. Confusion arises from the word having been applied to three different articles.

(1) A liripipe. 'With his typet ybound about his head' (Chaucer). 'thi typet as longe as a streamer that hangeth longe behinde and keepeth thee not hot' [1401].

(2) A cape. 'They be not all clerkes that have short typettes' [1481].

(3) A pendant from the elbow of the cote-hardie (q.s.).

TOLEY. Scarlet.

VAIR. Fur of grise made up in squares from back and belly of the animal.

VERMEL. Vermilion.

VOLUPERE. A nightcap, fourteenth century.

WADMOL. A coarse cloth.

WATCHET. A sort of blue cloth.

WEDE.
WEYD. } A garment.

Bibliography

(For convenience of reference the under-mentioned works are grouped according to their principal service for the student.)

1. *General, covering the whole of the Middle Ages (English) with illustrated text.*

MAX VON BOEHN. *Modes and Manners*. Vol. I. (Harrap, 1932.)

F. W. FAIRHOLT. *Costume in England* (2 vols. octavo) 4th edition 1909. The best of the smaller works; the volume 2 is a useful glossary.

DOROTHY HARTLEY. *Mediaeval Costume and Life* (Batsford, 1931).

HARTLEY and ELLIOT. *Life and Work of the People of England*, Vol. I. 'The Middle Ages' (Batsford, 1931).

WALTER OAKESHOTT. *The Sequence of English Mediaeval Art* (Faber and Faber, 1950).

J. R. PLANCHÉ. *Cyclopaedia and Dictionary of Costume* (2 vols. quarto) [1876].

HENRY SHAW. *Dresses and Decorations of the Middle Ages* (2 vols.) [1843].

F. M. KELLY and R. SCHWABE. *A Short History of Costume and Armour* from 1066–1800 [1931]. The mediaeval section has an excellent text, very reliable.

JOSEPH STRUTT. *Dress and Habits of the People of England* (2 vols. quarto) [1796] (Dates of some plates unreliable).
Manners and Customs (3 vols.) [1775].

2. *General, covering the Middle Ages in France.*

CAMILLE ENLART. *Le Costume* [Paris, 1927]. The careful analysis of details makes it invaluable for the English student where the costumes of the two countries correspond.

PAUL LACROIX. a. *Manners, Customs and Dress during the Middle Ages*. b. *The Arts in the Middle Ages*. c. *Science and Letters in the Middle Ages*. (Ed. 1877.)

CAMILLE PITON. *Le Costume Civil en France du XIII au XIX Siècle* (Paris, N.D.).

3. *Special Subject.*

E. R. GODDARD. *Women's Costume in French Texts of the Eleventh and Twelfth Centuries* (John Hopkins Press, Baltimore) [1927]. Contains a useful glossary of terms and textual quotations for a period insufficiently treated by most writers.

ADRIEN HARMAND. *Jeanne d'Arc, ses Costumes, son Armure* [Paris, 1927]. Dealing mainly with French costume of the fifteenth century, the author's exhaustive researches are nevertheless applicable in the main to England. A work which no serious student can afford to ignore.

EVA R. LUNDQUIST. *La Mode et son Vocabulaire de la mode féminine au moyen âge* [Goteborg, 1950]. Gives contemporary quotations from French and English sources of women's costume details in the Middle Ages.

C. OURSEL. *La Miniature du XII siècle.*

L'Abbaye de Citeaux. *D'Après Les Manuscrits de la Bibliothèque de Dijon.*

WALTER OAKESHOTT. *The Artists of the Winchester Bible.* (Faber and Faber, 1945.)

DOROTHY WHITELOCK. *Anglo-Saxon Wills.* (Cambridge University Press, 1930.)

4. *Books mainly of Illustrations.*

C. A. DAY and F. H. DINES. *Illustrations of Mediaeval Costume in England*, c. 1840.

H. W. LONSDALE and E. J. TARVER. *Illustrations of Mediaeval Costume* [1874]. Full of useful sketches from original sources. Slight text.

5. *Monumental Effigies.*

F. CHANCELLOR. *The Ancient Sepulchral Monuments of Essex,* [1890] (folio).

ALFRED FRYER. *Wooden Monumental Effigies in England and Wales* [1924].

A. GARDNER. *English Mediaeval Sculpture* [1937].
  Excellent illustrations from photographs.
  Alabaster Tombs [1940]. Also good illustrations.

RICHARD GOUGH. *Sepulchral Monuments in Great Britain* (4 vols. fol. 1786. Plates by Basire).

E. S. PRIOR and A. GARDNER. *Mediaeval Sculpture in England* [1912].

PRIOR and GARDNER. *Mediaeval Figure-Sculpture in England.* (Cambridge University Press, 1912.)

C. A. STOTHARD. *Monumental Effigies of Great Britain* (folio. New edition 1876). Superb plates giving accurate details of figures, invaluable for study.

6. *Brasses.*

C. BOUTELL. *Monumental Brasses,* [1849].

J. S. COTMAN. *Sepulchral Brasses in Norfolk* [folio, 1819].

H. DRUITT. *Costume in Brasses* [1906].

J. G. WALLER. *Monumental Brasses* (folio).

  (Brasses are instructive for costume details, but their alleged dates may mislead; sometimes they were made beforehand or years after the date of death, in the mode of the time of construction. But they show styles that were popular, especially among the merchant class.)

7. *Illuminated MSS.*

  A number, such as the Luttrell Psalter, Queen Mary's Psalter, etc. have been reproduced extensively, together with portions of others from the British Museum, the Bodleian Library and similar sources. These are, of course, invaluable for close study of details.

Sources of Illustrations

Frontispiece.

Matthew Paris. B.M. MS. Roy. 2A XXII.

1. (a) (Pseudo) 'Caedmon's Metrical Paraphrase of Scripture History'. Bodleian Library, Oxford. MS. Junius II. *c.* 1000.

    (b) and (c) The Benedictional of St. Aethelwold, *c.* 975. In the Library of the Duke of Devonshire.

    (d) Caedmon's Metrical Paraphrase.

2. (a) and (b) Carolingian Bible. B.M. MS. Add 10546. 9th Century.

    (c) The Benedictional of St. Aethelwold. C. 975.

3. (a) and (b) The Benedictional of St. Aethelwold.

4. All from Strutt.

    (a) B.M. MS. Cott. Tiberius B.V.

    (b) B.M. MS. Claud. B. IV.

    (c) B.M. MS. Cott. Claud. B. IV. (A composite drawing).

    (d) B.M. MS. Tiberius C. VI.

5. (a) The Bayeux Tapestry (late 11th C.).

    (b) B.M. MS. Cott. Claud. B. IV.

    The rest from Strutt.

    (c) B.M. MS. Claud. B. IV.

    (d) B.M. MS. Tiberius C. VI.

    (e) B.M. MS. Claud. 603.

    (f) B.M. MS. Tiberius C. VI.

6. All from Strutt.

    (a) B.M. MS. Harl. 2908.

    (b) B.M. MS. Claud. B. IV.

    (c) B.M. MS. Claud. B. IV.

7. (a) Winchester Bible, Winchester Cathedral Library.

    (b) B.M. MS. Nero C. IV. From Strutt. (A composite drawing.)

    (c) Winchester Bible.

    (d) B.M. MS. Cot. Nero C. VI. The St. Swithin Psalter.

    (e) Winchester Bible. (Figure in initial to Isaiah with buckle added from initial to Micah.)

8. (a) C. A. Stothard's 'Monumental Effigies of Great Britain'. (Effigies at Fontevraud).

    (b) J. R. Planché's 'Cyclopaedia of Costume', Vol. I.

    (c) and (d) B.M. MS. Cot. Nero C. VI. The St. Swithun Psalter.

(*e*) Winchester Bible.

(*f*) MS. Gough liturg. 2 f. 17. Bodleian Library, Oxford.

(*g*) and (*h*) From Strutt. B.M. MS. Nero C. IV.

(*i*) F. Hottenroth. Trachten.

9. (*a*) (*b*) (*e*) (*f*) and (*g*) The Bury St. Edmunds Bible, Corpus Christi College, Cambridge. MS. 2 f. 94.

(*c*) Guthlac Roll B.M. MS. Harl Roll Y.6.

(*d*) Bestiary. Ashmole MS. 1511f. Bodleian Library, Oxford.

10. (*a*) Rochester Cathedral, West Doorway. Neck line reconstructed from Chartres Cathedral Statues.

(*b*) Winchester Bible.

(*c*) The Bury St. Edmonds Bible, Corpus Christi College, Cambridge.

(*d*) B.M. Nero C. IV f. 15. Psalter from Winchester.

(*e*) From Strutt. B.M. MS. Nero. C. IV.

11. (*a*) From Strutt. Pl. XL.

(*b*) M.S. Bodley 269 (S.C. 1935) f.iii, Bodleian Library, Oxford.

(*c*) B.M. MS. Royal 2A XXII f.13b. Psalter of Westminster Abbey.

12. (*a*) B.M. MS. Sloane 2435 f.5.

(*b*) Bible Moralisée B.M. Facs. 169.

(*c*) Yates Thompson Lib. B.M. Facs. 183/3.

(*d*) From Strutt. Bod. 86 Arch. B.

13. (*a*) Matthew Paris. Corpus Christi College, Cambridge, MS. 26.

(*b*) and (*c*) Matthew Paris. B.M. MS. Cot. Nero D.I.

(*d*) Matthew Paris. Corpus Christi College, Cambridge, MS. 16.

(*e*) Matthew Paris. B.M. MS. Roy. 14 C. VII.

14. (*a*) (*b*) and (*c*) Pierpont Morgan MS. Facs.

(*d*) Matthew Paris. B.M. MS. Royal 14 C. VII.

(*e*) Matthew Paris, Corpus Christi College, Cambridge MS. 16.

(*f*) Planché's 'Cyclopaedia of Costume'. Vol. I.

15. (*a*) Matthew Paris, Corpus Christi College, Cambridge. MS. 16.

(*b*) B.M. MS. Add. 38116 (Huth. MS. iii) f. 11b. English Psalter.

(*c*) Matthew Paris, Corpus Christi College, Cambridge. MS. 26.

16. Effigy, Westminster Abbey. Aveline Countess of Lancaster. From C. A. Stothard's 'Monumental Effigies of Great Britain'.

17. (*a*) Bible Moralisée. B.M. Facs. 169.

(*b*) Camille Enlart's 'Le Costume'.

(*c*) 'Bible Historiée'. French MS. in The John Rylands Library, Manchester.

(*d*) Bible History, Moralised. B.M. MS. 18719 f.253b.

(*e*) Camille Enlart's 'Le Costume'.

(*f*) and (*g*) From Strutt. B.M. MS. Sloane 3983.

18. (*a*) Effigy, Scarcliff Church, Derbyshire. From Stothard.

(*b*) Chartres Cathedral. (North Porch).

19. (*a*) and (*d*) Luttrell Psalter, British Museum.

(*b*) B.M. MS. Addl. 12228.

(c) B.M. Bib. Reg. 19 D.ii.

20. (a) to (d) Luttrell Psalter, British Museum.

21. (a) Book of Gaston Phoebus Nat. Lib. of Paris. From Paul Lacroix's
'Manners, Customs and Dress during the Middle Ages'.

(b) (c) (d) and (e) Luttrell Psalter, British Museum.

(f) and (g) Queen Mary's Psalter, British Museum.

22. (a) Wall Painting, Claverley, Shropshire.

(b) (c) and (d) B.M. MS. Roy. 19 B. XV.

(e) Brass, St. Stephen's Church, Norwich. From J. S. Cotman's 'Sepulchral
Brasses in Norfolk'.

(f) Brass, St. Margaret's Church, Kings Lynn. From Cotman.

23. (a) B.M. MS. Arundel 83, Psalter of Robert de Lisle.

(b) and (c) Luttrell Psalter, British Museum.

24. (a) to (e) From the Luttrell Psalter.

25. (a) to (h) excluding (c) From the Luttrell Psalter, British Museum.

(c) B.M. MS. Add. No. 10292 f.55. From H. Haines' 'Manual of Monumental Brasses', Part. 1.

26. (a) to (e) The Luttrell Psalter, British Museum.

27. (a) to (e) The Luttrell Psalter, British Museum.

28. (a) and (b) Queen Mary's Psalter, British Museum.

(c) An English Mediaeval Sketch-book, No. 1916, in the Pepsyan Library,
Magdalene College, Cambridge.

29. (a) and (b) The Luttrell Psalter, British Museum.

(c) B.M. MS. Arundel 83 f. 124. Psalter of Robert, Baron de Lisle.

(d) Queen Mary's Psalter, British Museum.

(e) Figure on a band of embroidered red velvet, c. 1310. Victoria and
Albert Museum.

30. (a) and (b) From Strutt. B.M. MS. Roy. 15 D. ii.

(c) and (d) The Luttrell Psalter, British Museum.

31. (a) Brass, South Acre Church, Norfolk. From Cotman.

(b) Brass, St. Margaret's Church, Kings Lynn. From Cotman.

32. (a) Effigy of William of Hatfield, York Minster.

(b) Wooden effigy of Walter de Helyon, Much Marcle, Herefordshire.

33. (a) From Adrien Harmand's 'Jeanne d'Arc'.

(b) Weeper on Tomb of Sir Roger de Kerdeston, Reepham Church,
Norfolk. From C. A. Stothard.

(c) Planche's 'Cyclopaedia of Costume', Vol. 1.

34. (a) From Strutt, B.M. MS. 20 B. vii.

(b) Contemporary portrait of the Black Prince, from a Royal Pedigree
parchment roll.

(c) From Camille Enlart's 'Le Costume'.

(d) From Fairholt's 'Costume in England', Vol. 1.

(e) and (f) B.M. MS. Roy. 20B. VI f.2. Epistle of P. de Naizieres to
Richard II of England.

35. (a) Brass, St. Margaret's Church, Kings Lynn. From Cotman.
    (b) From Strutt. Liber Regalis in the Abbey Library at Westminster.
    (c) Window in Winchester Cathedral.
    (d) to (h) Planche's 'Cyclopaedia of Costume', Vol. 1. Originally drawn from wall-paintings in St. Stephen's Chapel, Westminster.
36. (a) (b) (c) (d) and (f) Diagrams.
    (e) From Strutt. Liber Regalis in the Abbey Library at Westminster.
    (g) From Strutt. B.M. MS. Roy. 20 C. VII.
    (h) B.M. MS. Roy. 20 C. VII. Chroniques de St. Denis.
37. (a) Brass, Winterbourne Church, Glos. From C. Boutell's 'Monumental Brasses of England'.
    (b) Brass, once in Ingham Church, Norfolk. From Stothard.
    (c) Jeanne de Bourbon. Part of the Narbonne 'Parement' Louvre.
    (d) From the tomb of Edward III, Westminster Abbey.
38. (a) Effigy, St. Mary's Church, Warwick. From Gough.
    (b) Jeanne d'Armagnac, Palais de Justice, Poitiers.
39. (a) Brass, Wood Ditton Church, Camb. From C. Boutell's 'Monumental Brasses of England'.
    (b) Brass, Spilsby Church, Lincs. From C. Boutell.
    (c) Effigy, East Harling Church, Norfolk.
40. (a) Effigy, Canterbury Cathedral. From Stothard.
    (b) Effigy, Atherington Church, Devon. From Stothard.
41. (a) Brass, Ore Church, Sussex.
    (b) Brass, Northleach Church, Glos.
    (c) Brass, Kingston-upon-Thames Church, Surrey.
    All from Boutell.
42. (a) Les Très Riches Heures du Duc de Berry.
    (b) and (c) Brussels MS. 9466 fol. 1. Martin le Franc et Philippe le Bon.
    (d) and (f) B.M. MS. Roy. 20 C. VII.
    (e) From Harmand. An English Falkoner.
43. (a) Alabaster Slab.
    (b) Weeper on tomb at Elford Church.
    (c) From the 'Planet Venus'. Franco-Burgundian School.
    (d) John Foxton's 'Cosmography', Trinity College, Cambridge.
    (e) From Shaw. B.M. MS. Arundel, No. 38.
44. (a) and (b) From a panel of the Hardwicke Tapestries reproduced in the 'Connoisseur', May-Aug. 1902.
    (c) Mural Panel. Hospice Belle Ypres.
45. (a) From Jean Fouquet. The Martyrdom of St. Apollonia.
    (b) From Adrien Harmand's 'Jeanne d'Arc'.
    (c) From a photograph of the tapestry in the Burrell Collection.
    (d) and (e) From Adrien Harmand's 'Jeanne d'Arc'.
    N.B. (a) (b) (c) and (d) although taken from sources belonging to the 2nd half of the 15th century, are equally illustrative of the styles of the 1st half.

SOURCES OF ILLUSTRATIONS

46. (*a*) and (*d*) From Harmand's 'Jeanne d'Arc'.
    (*b*) From a photograph of the tapestry in the Burrell Collection.
    (*c*) Brass, St. Stephen's Church, Norwich. From Cotman.
    (*e*) J. van Eyck.
    (*f*) From Planche's 'Cyclopaedia of Costume', Vol. 1.
47. (*a*) Lydgate's 'Sege of Troye'. The John Rylands Library, Manchester.
    (*b*) and (*e*) Les Très Riches Heures du Duc de Berry.
    (*c*) (*f*) and (*g*) B.M. MS. Roy. 20 C. VII.
    (*d*) From Harmand.
48. (*a*) to (*d*) J. Van Eyck.
49. (*a*) Brass, St. Giles Church, Norwich. From Cotman.
    (*b*) and (*d*) From Harmand.
    (*c*) Les Très Riches Heures du Duc de Berry.
    (*e*) Effigy, Lingfield Church, Surrey.
50. (*a*) Ashwelthorpe Church, Norfolk. From Stothard.
    (*b*) From Paul Lacroix.
51. (*a*) Brass, Tilbrook Church, Bedfordshire.
    (*b*) Brass, Sawtry Church, Huntingdonshire.
    (*c*) Brass, Castle Donington Church, Leicestershire.
    All three from Boutell's 'Monumental Brasses'.
52. (*a*) Brass, Spilsby Church, Lincolnshire. From Boutell's 'Monumental Brasses'.
    (*b*) B.M. MS. Roy. 20 C. VII.
    (*c*) Brass, Bedinton Church, Surrey. From Boutell's 'Monumental Brasses'.
    (*d*) and (*e*) B.M. MS. Harl. 4431.
53. Brass of Joyce, Lady Tiptoft, Enfield Church, Middlesex. From Boutell's 'Monumental Brasses'.
54. (*a*) From Harmand.
    (*b*) From a Burrell tapestry, photograph.
    (*c*) Brass, Ormesby Church, Norfolk. From Cotman.
55. (*a*) Brass, Felbrigg Church, Norfolk. From Cotman.
    (*b*) Effigy, Over Peover Church, Cheshire.
    (*c*) Effigy, Lingfield Church, Surrey.
56. Jan Van Eyck. Portrait of his wife.
57. Effigy, Ashwelthorpe Church, Norfolk. From Stothard.
58. (*a*) Effigy, Hoveringham Church, Notts. From Stothard.
    (*b*) Effigy, Wingfield Church, Suffolk. From Stothard.
59. (*a*) Jeanne de Montejean. (Indre-et-Loire.)
    (*b*) Peter Christus. The Nativity.
    (*c*) Effigy, Arundel, Sussex.
60. (*a*) Jean Fouquet.
    (*b*) and (*d*) Wall Paintings in Eton College Chapel.
    (*c*) From Strutt. Plate CXXVII.

(e) Jean Fouquet and successor. The Building of the Roman Wall.
61. (a) Master of King René.
    (b) B.M. MS. Roy. 15 E. IV.
62. (a) J. Mielot et Philippe le Bon.
    (b) The Vision of St. Bernadinus. French School.
    (c) From Strutt. B.M. MS. Cott. Nero D. IX.
63. (a) Jean Fouquet.
    (b) From Strutt. B.M. MS. Roy. 15 E. IV.
    (c) Miniature from the 'Livres des Comptes'.
64. (a) From Shaw. B.M. MS. Harl. 4425.
    (b) Master of Moulins.
65. (a) Jean Fouquet. Etienne Chevalier.
66. (a) Master of King René.
    (b) Fritz Herlin.
    (c) Camille Pitou. 'Le Costume Civil en France'.
    (d) From Planché's 'Cyclopaedia of Costume', Vol. 1.
    (e) Dirk Bouts, Brussels.
67. (a) Chroniques de Philippe le Bon.
    (b) and (d) Gerard David.
    (c) From Planché's 'Cyclopaedia of Costume', Vol. 1.
68. (a) From Planché. B.M. MS. Cott. Julius IV.
    (b) From Shaw. B.M. MS. Cott. Julius E. IV.
69. (a) A portrait of Edward IV, a painting belonging to the Society of
        Antiquaries.
    (b) Dirk Bouts. Portrait of a Man. National Gallery.
70. (a) Effigy, Norbury Church, Derby.
    (b) Jean Fouquet. Portrait of Charles VII.
71. (a) Loyset Liedet, Brussels, MS. 9967 f.39.
    (b) and (c) Wall Paintings in Eton College Chapel.
72. (a) Peinture murale du XVe siècle, Palais du Trocadéro, Paris.
    (b) Brass, West Herling Church, Norfolk. From Cotman.
    (c) Wall Painting in Eton College Chapel.
73. (a) French Tapestry.
    (b) B.M. MS. Roy. 16 F. II f.188.
74. (a) M. S. Douce 213, Bodleian Library, Oxford.
    (b) Wall Painting, Eton College, Chapel.
    (c) From Strutt. B.M. MS. Roy. 15 E. VI
    (d) Effigy, Brancepeth Church, Durham. From Stothard.
75.   Peter Christus. Portrait of a Young Woman.
76. (a) Peter Christus. The Legend of St. Eloi.
    (b) Brass, Shernbourn Church, Norfolk. From Cotman.
    (c) Brass, Iselham Church, Cambridgeshire. From Gough.
77. (a) Roger Van der Weyden. Portrait of a Lady.

(*b*) Burgundian School. Portrait of Guillemotte de Vergy. Worcester, U.S.A. Art Museum.

78. (*a*) The Adoration of the Child, Avignon, Musée Calvet.

    (*b*) B.M. MS. Roy. 16 f.ii.

    (*c*) Brass, Merton Church, Norfolk. From Cotman.

79.   Duchess Anne de Bourbon, from the Moulins Triptych.

Index

(*See* Glossary for terms not defined in the text and for list of materials and colours not directly referred to in the text. Additional sources and references are contained in the Bibliography. Glossary, pages 169 to 175. Bibliography, pages 176 to 178. For sources of illustrations, *see* pages 179 to 185).

Italicised figures are page references to illustrations or Plate references to the four illustrations in colour.

INDEX

Cat fur, 105
Cauls, *165*, 166, *167*
Ceremonial mantles, 83, 106, 122, *123*
Chamlet, 139
Chaperons, *112*, 113, *137* seqq., *140*, 147
Chaplet headdress, 125
Chaucer, 78, 83, 89, 92, 95
Chimney-pot styles, *160*, 161
Circotte, 167
Circular roll headdress, 128, *Pl. 52*
Civet, 105
Clasps, 11; *see* Jewellery
Clean-shaving, 47, 65, 89, 119, 150
Cloaks, 72, 83, 106, 144; *see* Mantles
Clogs, 14, 18
Closed gown (early houppelande), 100
Closed sleeves, 103, 139, *Pl. 43*; buttoned, 69, 90, 103; German mode, 103
Close-fitting kirtle bodice, 69, 90
Cloth of gold, 143
Coat (jacket synonym), 141
Codpieces, 108, *135*, 144, *145*
Coifs, 34, *45*, *46*, 47, *63*, 65, 87, 115
Collars, 121, *143*, 155; bertha, 155, 157; bottle-neck, 102, *Pl. 52*; houppelande, typical *122*, stand-up, V-front, *143*. See *Pl. 43*, *Pl. 52*
Colours, 12th c., 31; 14th c., 97; 15th c., of hoods, 113; of hats, 117; of hose, 109; women's, 18, 133
Coney fur, 105
Coronets, *93*, 95, *123*, *132*, 167; with bosses, *see* Fillets; with caul, *167*; with plaits, *93*; with templers, templettes, *123*, *132*
Cote, *see* Super-tunic
Cote-hardie, *57*, *58*, *79*, *84*, *91*; early 15th c., 100, 120; introduction of, 57; late 14th c., changes in, 80; replacement of, by jacket, 136; second half of 14th c., variations, 90; variations of, for peasants and gentry, 57, *58*; with dagged tippets, *84*; with short tippets, *Pl. 52*; with fitchets and long tippets, *91*; with long tippets, 90, *91*
Cotton MS, 37, 41, *161*
Coudières, 80
Cow-hide, for boots, 109
Crespines (cauls), 53, 74, *75*, 95, 166
Criss-cross leg bandages, *21*, *22*
Cropped hair: bowl, *99*, *114*, *116*, 117, *143*, 150; short, 117
Crowns (queen's), 18, 40
Cuffs: at elbow, 80; narrowing of, 42; turn-back, 20, 28. See Sleeves
Cushion headdress, *91*, 95, 125
Cuthbert, Saint, 15
Cylindrical sleeves, 102, 103, 155

Daggers, *67*, 68, 89, 106, 119, 133; on belt, 106; on shoulder-belt, *99*, *118*
Dagging, 35, 80, 82, 83, 97; decline of, 83; on cote-hardies, 80, *84*; on houppelandes, 82, 83, *84*, 105; on mantles, *79*, *81*; on sleeves, 82, *112*; on unbelted huke, *104*; widely fashionable period of, 83. *See Pl. 43*
Damask, 100, 105, 113; with woven patterns, designs of, 105
Decorated hat bands, vogue of, 89
Deep skull caps, 115
Demi-ceint, 168
Demi-gown, unbelted, *141*
Detachable sleeves, 134
Double mantles, 11, 18, 26, *Pl. 6*
Doublet, 55, 98–100; and stomacher, *135*; early 15th c. styles of, 98–100; later 15th c. variations of, 134
Drawers, *see* Braies
Dressing-gowns, mantles used as, 50
Duck-billed shoes, 147

Edward I, 47
Edward II, 62
Edward III, 85
Edward IV, 134, 136
Eleanor, Queen, 53
Elizabeth of York, Henry VII's wife, 161, 166
Embroidered belt, later 15th c., 155
Embroidery, 9, 15, 35 and *passim*; on aprons, 74, 77; on belts, 155; on 14th c. shoes, 62, *63*; on gloves, *43*, *46*, 68; on gorget band, 65; on hose, 144; on houppelandes, *101*, 105; jewelled and spangled, 133; on Kirtle, *16*, *17*, *19*, *154* *and passim*; on male garb, 11, *20*, *21*, 35, *43*, *63*, *and see* Dagging, *also* Frontispiece; Saxon, 16; on 13th c. tunics, *43*
'English work', 19
Epaulettes, 83, *101*
Ermine, 161; with black tails, 105
Estaches, 78, 83
Eulogium Historiarum, 85, 87, 113
Eyebrow plucking, 97, 131
Eyelet holes, 108, 111; *see also* Points, 108

Face painting, 97, 131; with rouge, 41
False hair, 12th c., use of, 40
'Fashionable posture', late 14th c., 97
Fastenings: bodice, 155, 157; brimmed hats, 33–4, *116*, 117, *and see* Liripipes; buttons as, 55, *56*, 57, *79*, 80, *81*, 82, *84*, *and see* Sleeves; cloaks, boots, 87, 10, 11, 31, 37, *99*; cord and ring, 22, 31; corner and ring, 31; cord 'en coulisse', 13, 22, 31; cotehardie, 80, 90; doublet, 98, 134;

187

INDEX

Low-collared cape, 60
Low-necked jacket, *137*
Lydgate, 152

Magyar (type) sleeves, 28, *32, and see* Frontispiece
Mahoitres, 136, *140*, 155
Mantles, 92, 161; *see* Ceremonial mantles, Double mantles, Frontispiece
Marten fur, 117, 143, 160
Materials: all-over patterned, 20; of belts, early 15th c., 105; of bonnets, early mediaeval, 14; of boots, 14, 109; of braies, 31; of buttons, 55; of cloak linings, 60; of cloaks, 31; of doublets, 100, 134; of girdles, 36, 38, *and see* Girdles; of gowns, 142, 143; of hats, 117, *and see* Hats; of head-rails, 18; of headdresses, 15th c., 127; of hooded cloaks, 22; of hood-turbans, 113; of hose, 22, 26, *and see* Hose variations; of jackets, later 15th c., 139; of houppelandes, 105; of shoes, 14, 33, 147, *and see* Shoes; of stockings, 13th c., 50; of tunics, 35; of wimples, 40; principal uses of broad-cloth, 100; finer materials, early, 31; fur, 65 *and see* Furs; fustian, 100, 139, 141; haircloth, 19; leather, 14, 24, 31, 35, 147, *and see* Shoes, etc.; linen, 9, 14, 16, 19, 31, 34, 35, 40, 53, 95; silk, 11, 33, 35, 40, 50, 105, 127; taffeta, 65, 105, 166; velvet, 100, 105, 113, 134, 139, 141, 143, 147, 164; wool, 9, 14, 16, 22, 35, 105, 168, *and see* named garments
Metal: fillets, 14, 34, *37*; with wimple, 39; half-bands, 38, 40
Men's garments and styles: by centuries; 9th and 10th, 9–15; 11th, 20–5; 12th, 28–35; 13th, 42–7; 14th, early, 55–68; 14th, later, 78–89; 15th, early, 98–119; 15th, later, 134–52; accessories, 14, 25, 34, 47, 65, 89, 119, 152; belts, importance of, 105; braies, 13, 108; 13; cloaks, mantles, 11, 22, 31, 44, 144; eleventh c., 22; hooded, 22; of nobles, 22; small fur-lined, 31; colours, 15; cote-hardie, 57, 58, 60, 80, 100; double mantle, 11; doublet, 98, 134, *135*; fitchet, 44; foot-wear, 13, 24, 33, 44, 62, 85, 109, *110*, 144, *146*, 147, *148*; garnache, 60, 82; gipon, 55, 57, *56*; gloves, *30*, 34, 46; gown, 142, *143*; hair styles, 14, 24–5, 34, 47, 65, 89, 116, 117, 119, 150, *151*; headwear, 14, 33, *45*, 47, 62, 64, 65, 87, *88*, 89, 111, *112*, 113, *114*, 115, 117, 147, *149*; hose, *see* Legwear; houppelandes, 82, 99, *100*, 102, 103, 105, *see* Gown; huke, 143–4; jacket after 1500, 136–40, 141; jewels, *30*, 34, 35, *and see* Accessories; leg wear, 13, 23,

31, 60, 83, 85, 106; outer garments, 5, 60, 83, 106; peasant garb, 13th c., *46*; petticoat or waistcoat, 136; pourpoint, *see* Gipon; supertunic, 9–11, 20, 21, 28–31, 42; new style of 13th c., 42, 44; tunic, 9, 16, 20, 29, 42, 55. *See* named garments for references to illustrations
Miniver, 117, 125, 160
Mokador, *see* Muckinder
Mourning: hood, 125, 166; 15th c., 166–7; later 14th c., 89
Moustache without beard, 34
Muckinder, 152

Nebula headdress, *93, 95*, 131
Necklaces, *123*, 133, 152, *162, Pl. 43*
Necklines, 9, 11, 16, 28, 36, 48, 57, 69, 98 seqq., 112, 136 seqq., 155 seqq.; cote-hardie, 14th c., 57; cote-hardie, 15th c., 100; doublet, early 15th c., 98; doublet, later 15th c., 134; furred, later 15th c., 151; gown, 155, 157; houppelande, earlier, 102, 103; later, 122; jacket, later 15th c., 136; kirtle, 12th c., 36; low necked jacket, *137*; sideless surcoat, 92; twelfth c. innovations, 28; V-shaped, 36, 48, *112*, wide-slit, 48, 69
Nobility, styles confined to, 11, 14, 22, 28, 33, 34, 35, 47, 62, 68, 77, 85, 100, 103, 105, 122, 133, 136, 139, 143, 147, 157, 160, 161, 166, 167, 168

Occleve, Thomas, 105
Odeham, Margaret, 157
Open sleeves, 103, 139
Ornamental stocking borders, 24, 31
Over-garments, *see* Men's, Women's
Over-stockings, *141*, 144, *145*

Padded roll, 115. *See* Cushion, *and Pl. 52*
Padding of doublet, 98; of gipons, 78
Pads in hair, 117
Page-boy crop, 150
Pantofles (mules), 147
Parti-coloured hose, 60, *81 84*, 85, 109, 144
Paston, M., 157
Pattens, 87, *101*, 110, 111, *138*, 146, 147, *154*, 168; leather and wooden, later 15th c., *146*
Patterns of houppelande materials, 105
Peasants' garments and styles, 13, 22, *46, 56, 59, 66, 67*, 68, 74, 105, *107*, 110, 111, *116*, 124, 125, 145
Pedestrian huke, 106
Pelissons: introduction of, 31; fur-lined, 48; short, 72, 92
Penner and inkhorn, 68
Petticoat, man's, 136
Phrygian bonnets, 14, *23, 24, 32, 33*

190